THE
Archive Photographs
SERIES

CENTRAL
GLASGOW

Paterson's shop at 1,256 Argyle Street on an autumn day in 1923 and there is much bad news in the papers - does anything change? The Polmont mine disaster, one of the worst ever, killed 40 men by flooding on 26 September but 8 days later 5 trapped survivors were brought up. They had lived on water for a week and had made their wills. They were cheerful but 'dying for a fag'. *Forward*, the socialist weekly, and D.C. Thomson's *Weekly News* are full of details about what happened at No. 23 Redding pit, and why. The owners were James Nimmo & Co. of Glasgow. The *Glasgow Herald's* main item 'Bavaria Defies Berlin' is about a campaign by that state to break away from the Reich and be a kingdom again; there is also mention in the piece of a troublemaker called Adolf Hitler and rumours that he is planning a 'putsch'. In the *Daily Herald* Ramsay Macdonald, very soon to be Prime Minister, writes about the workless. No wonder A.G. Gardner is asking 'Is Life Worth Living?' *The People's Friend*, never a herald of doom and gloom, would say yes and is offering a 'Great Free Pattern.' Paterson stocks 'All Books for Overnewton Public School' and also sells 'Tramway Two Stage Tokens'. Dobie of Paisley is another famous name, their Four Square tobacco and cigarettes fated to disappear after the war. The window on the right is a veritable picture gallery of prints and postcards, getting much attention. Number 1,256 was damaged by a nearby bomb in 1941 and after the war was reduced to one storey. It is now a public house. (The Eaglesham Archive, courtesy of Bob Rhodes)

THE
Archive Photographs
SERIES

CENTRAL
GLASGOW

Compiled by
Peter Stewart

CHALFORD

The Chalford Publishing Company
St Mary's Mill, Chalford,
Stroud, Gloucestershire, GL6 8NX

ISBN 0 7524 0675 2

Typesetting and origination by
The Chalford Publishing Company
Printed in Great Britain by
Bailey Print, Dursley, Gloucestershire

Cover Illustration:
A topping-out ceremony behind the City Chambers around 1914.

Contents

Map of Central Glasgow in the 1930s.

Introduction

Glasgow welcomed the twentieth century with a flourish. The 1901 International Exhibition showed who was still the Empire's Second City and since then a few more such shows have been staged. Though the world may have forgotten those joyous events, they became firmly woven into the local folk memory. But Glasgow's reputation for civic pride and enjoyment went along with a name for other sorts of things, which did it no good at all in the middle years of this century.

Photographs show the city centre and a bit beyond, into parts which once seemed to be all grimy tenements, little shops and tramlines. Most are of this century. The images cannot show every favourite scene, but give a flavour of the place and its people and they remind us of what has changed and what, to the relief of many, has not. No nostalgic lament for old times, but a reminder of what once was. Even in pre-war days when nothing much seemed to happen, time was not standing still. Social change and advance in technology forever alter the way we live and the look of the city. In recent years, though, the pace of change has been much faster and more violent. The Empire is no more and the Second City another place - but who wants to be second anyway? Glasgow has been No Mean City, City of Culture. Cancer of the Empire too and soon, City of Architecture and Design. After St Mungo came and put his church beside the Molendinar in the sixth century, Glasgow began to grow, but by 1901 was still compact with no substantial surrounding urban sprawl.

Compared to a modern local authority, Glasgow, a finger in every pie, was almost a City State - and a very good one. In 1896, a Vienna paper advised that it was 'a waste of time and money' to study municipal organisation anywhere else, 'for Glasgow stands, as far as communal life and government goes, at the top of civilisation.' The *Municipal Enterprise Handbook* of 1904 lists everything you might need, from Art Galleries to Weights and Measures, by way of Markets (eight, plus three slaughter houses) the Inebriates' Reformatory and Model Lodging Houses. Life for many could still be grim, but it was after the First World War that Glasgow really fell on hard times.

The 1930s Depression hit hard and brought more misery. Glasgow was quite unjustly known as an unsafe city where razor gangs roamed the streets, the pavements littered with torpid drunks. The term 'Red Clydeside' was proudly voiced by those who felt it enhanced the city's fame. Glaswegians were depicted as bigoted, bolshie and prone to over-indulgence. A strange sentimental longing for the old days lingers on for some, as though there were not enough new problems.

By 1945, in a city of well over a million, the bad housing and overcrowding were notorious. The well intentioned removal of many of the younger and productive to soulless estates and

New Towns, and the somewhat greater allure of Australia and Canada, did still more damage to a city to which war, for all its hardships, had given renewed life. Only recently has Glasgow woken up to its new role as a post-industrial city and seen itself as a vibrant centre of commerce, education and the arts, and a prime tourist attraction.

Glasgow today is a cleaner, less crowded city. True, many of the new buildings could be anywhere. Gone are the trams, once so indispensable, removed to speed up the traffic. Gone, bar one, are the dozen stores of the mighty House of Fraser and most other locally owned city centre shops. Gone are the secondhand book barrows. You can dine out better than you ever could before, but whatever happened to Daniel Brown's and Miss Rombach's? Yet still the city retains its distinctive character. There are not a few fine modern developments in the centre, (and some which few can praise) and much Victorian splendour survives. And, of course, Charles Rennie Macintosh.

Glasgow city centre enjoys a magnificent site, climbing steeply from the Clyde, a river wide enough to display its several handsome bridges. The rise to Garnethill, the east-west slope and the grid pattern allow for some striking vistas which the Victorians realised. The M8, looping closely round the centre before soaring across the Clyde is used, and verbally abused, in equal measure; it is hard to imagine how Glasgow could cope without it, but no one can divide a city by an elevated motorway without leaving wastelands beneath and around, and scars remain.

Many of the photographs are from picture postcards. They show not merely the stones of a city, but its life, people coming and going or just there to stand and stare. Scenes taken in busy city centre streets, or in quieter ones beyond, show our forbears (or contemporaries) going about their business in surroundings often familiar but changed enough to look archaic.

Today's Glaswegians are much the same as any other Britons - a mixed bunch whose origins include many parts of the globe. Most get on together quite well and have not been seen out on the streets, rioting, burning and looting. Those who appear here were of the city at the time. Industries which once employed thousands have, if they survived at all, moved away to less expensive and congested parts. The city centre is now more a place for commerce and many of the small businesses in the clothing, food and other trades, dotted around the centre, are gone. Modern industry, rightly regulated in the interests of health and safety, needs space - though not so many people.

Much verse was written last century in praise of Glasgow (that by McGonagall was but by a short head the worst.) Earlier this century Dundee's Will Fyffe sang a few lines worthy of immortality. *I Belong to Glasgow* remains the proudest boast those born here could imagine, and *Glasgow Belongs to Me* their proudest claim.

Acknowledgements

I have had much help with permission to reproduce photographs and I apologise to any copyright holders I have not been able to trace. Individual acknowledgment will be found in brackets at the end of the captions. Many of the postcards (PPCs) were by J.Valentine & Sons of Dundee; the Valentine Archive is now at the University of St Andrews Library whose staff have been particularly helpful. Much historical information has also been given freely by those I have asked. I thank all who have helped me in various ways, including Gordon Carroll, Anthony Duda, George Gardner, Stanley Hunter, Jimmy Logan OBE, Julia McLeod, John Maxton MP, John Moore, James Murray, Bob Rhodes, John Stewart, Joyce Stewart, Alma Topen, John Gorevan and George Gardner of the University of Glasgow Archives and the staffs of the Mitchell Library and Glasgow Archives. David Buxton, senior editor at Chalford Publishing has, as before, been most helpful to me throughout. My wife, Margaret has helped with checking the typescript and with her encouragement.

One

Around Glasgow Cross

The Cross was the heart of the city until the start of the steady westward movement of people, business and town council, which got under way about two hundred years ago. Glasgow was then quite small but well laid out, with good public buildings which mightily impressed visitors. History had been made here in a turbulent past. William Wallace gave Edward I a bloody nose hereabouts in 1300, James Watt had his epoch-making inspiration while walking on the Green and Bonnie Prince Charlie got a distinctly cool welcome when he turned up. No one could then take liberties with the people and get away with it. When things got too hot, the military were at hand in the guard post in the Saltmarket (later at the foot of Candleriggs) and their barracks were not far away. Up High Street was the University and the Cathedral, where Glasgow had had its beginnings. South, the Saltmarket led to the Briggate and the old bridge. Westward was the short stretch of Trongate, and eastward the Gallowgate, leading to the site of much summary justice. And that, more or less, was it. While Glasgow ruled the tobacco trade the city's wealthy 'Tobacco Lords' took the air in the Trongate and the lesser breeds had to step aside, but after that boom ended this part of the city became decidedly unpopular with the well-to-do. Until about the 1820s the Glasgow mob was something to be feared, and over the centuries many a riot or battle took place by the Cross between the people and the guardians of law and order. The streets around the Cross became a warren of foul, crumbling old tenements, a place of crime, disease and unspeakable stench. The University upped and left in 1870 and a slum clearance scheme removed the worst of the housing. A few relics of old times remain but most of the district is Victorian or later. Much has been done in recent days to alter the neglected air that has long blighted this end of the city centre and to make the most of the fine group of buildings at Glasgow Cross. The inspired Merchant City plans, not yet fully realised, promise much more. The near East End takes in the ancient Green by the Clyde and Bridgeton Cross and had some of the city's worst housing.

Glasgow Cross in the 1930s and in the '60s. The Tolbooth Steeple (1626) survives traffic planners' efforts to remove it. It was connected to the much admired Tontine building and *piazza* taken down in 1814. Left, is the entrance to Glasgow Cross station on the LMS Low Level from Rutherglen, closed in 1964, reopened (but not this station) in 1979 as the electrified Argyle Line to Dalmuir and points west. Below, a trolleybus on route 102 to Riddrie has replaced the tram. A British Rail 'mechanical horse' is crossing into Saltmarket. The sign of the clog is at John Moffat's shoe shop, opened in 1843 but these days, although the general picture remains much the same, trolleybuses, horses, living or otherwise, and the clog are long gone. (PPC, *National Series*, Millar & Lang)

The Mercat Cross is a worthy 1929 reproduction of an earlier one which was last seen in 1659. The impressive Mercat Building, from the same decade, happily survives much as before. The goods line crossing the picture remains, but not the church on the right. (PPC, *Caledonia Series*)

The fish market, 1913, in the Briggate (the ancient route from the cross to the river) was built in 1873. It replaced the Merchant's House of 1659, the fine tiered steeple of which remains. In 1986 it became a shopping centre with a mix of food, crafts and the like, but it was in the wrong place and was soon in trouble. The building, beautifully restored, awaits another use. (PPC)

London Road in 1911. We can tell the date from a poster on the gable end above the bridge. It advertises 'Exhibition Salmon,' 1911 being the year of the third Kelvingrove Exhibition. Whitbread's beer is shown above the salmon - no doubt they would go down well together. In the extreme right foreground, at No.16, is the Swiss Restaurant, while next door the sign reads 'Public House Trust.' There were two of these short lived 'reformed' pubs in Glasgow, with managers who were meant to provide soft drinks and food as well as alcohol - an idea before its time, at least for this city. (PPC, *Caledonia Series*, Julia McLeod Collection)

King Billy in close up, on his plinth, seated there on his horse since 1734. He was moved from here to High Street in 1933, having already been moved a little way up the Trongate at an earlier date.

A view from the London Road corner showing, left, Glasgow Cross station, seemingly renamed Eldorado, though that was merely an advert for a popular South African tonic wine. Britannia, with trident, looks down from the top of the warehouse on the right on a June day in 1936. A white coated policeman stands in front of the Commercial Bank of Scotland. In the right foregound a group of women have their baskets of washing, bound, no doubt, for the steamie. (PPC, Copyright J.Salmon Ltd, Sevenoaks, Kent, reproduced with their kind permission from an image in my collection ©)

GLASGOW CROSS 12631

Trongate from Glasgow Cross, *c.* 1912. William of Orange points to the Tron church of 1594, burnt down in 1793 during a Hell Fire Club drunken revel. The steeple, added in 1631, survived for a new church to be built behind it after the fire. Gas light illuminated the clock faces as early as 1823. Long roofless, it is now the Tron Theatre. The shops seen behind the statue are A.J. Carroll & Co at No.37 and Arthur's (clothiers) at No.39. (PPC, E. & A. Schwerdtfeger, E0232)

Trongate, *c.* 1910, looking towards the Cross, with King Street opening on the right. The Scotch Clothing Company has its windows crammed full of bargains. Next door are the Tron Tea Rooms, a short lived enterprise. A Caledonian Railway Passenger Train parcel's van is doing a U turn round the policeman in this busy scene. (PPC, Judges Ltd, Hastings, 1897)

14

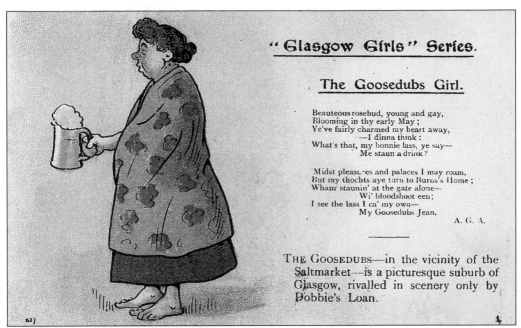

The Goosedubs Girl - one of a set of Edwardian satirical postcards. Goosedubs is an ancient lane between Stockwell Street and the Bridgegate. The series title Glasgow Girls was a take-off of the Glasgow Boys, the school of painters; ironically their female contemporaries are now known as the Glasgow Girls. (PPC, *National Series*)

Great Hamilton Street, now London Road, at Kent Street, 1912. St Alphonsus church, still in use, dates from 1905 and replaced the original, opened here in 1846 when many Irish Roman Catholics were arriving in Glasgow. Fox the florist 'from Lamb's Pass' is on the right and at the provision shop in Kent Street you can get your 'Marshall's Semolina'. Lamb's Pass has gone, but the Schipka Pass, commemorating the Bulgarian battle of 1877 when, with Russian help they beat the Turks, remains nearby, housing a small secondhand market. (PPC, *Caledonia Series*, Julia McLeod Collection)

Paddy's Market was the exchange and mart for Irish immigrants last century, always to be found in the Bridgegate area and finishing up here by the railway arches. Many attempts have been made to see it on its way but it remains as a Glasgow institution. This photograph is as recent as ten years ago. The centre arch houses The Mad Fryer just in case you feel like lunch.

This is Barrowland. The 'Barras', Glasgow's traditional weekend market for mainly secondhand clothes, furniture and bric-a-brac, has long been famous, though old timers will tell you that, like anything else you can name, it's not what it was. It still draws its crowds though, including, on occasion, the police and the customs and excise. The Barrowland Ballroom has enjoyed equal fame. We are looking along Kent Street from Gallowgate, with Moncur Street behind the van which is displaying works of art at an affordable price. It is June 1974.

Opposite: Boarding the No.29 tram for Maryhill in Gallowgate on a Saturday afternoon around 1960. Ross Street, connecting with London Road, is on the left. Ahead is Glasgow Cross and behind us is Barrowland and most of the people here will have been at the market.

RIVER CLYDE AT GLASGOW GREEN, GLASGOW.   B.4241

Glasgow Green, the city's ancient common, has long been jealously guarded from those with other plans. Once it stretched to Jamaica Street but at the far end, Fleshers' Haugh was added in 1792. A place for rallies, parades and protests, James Maxton (see page 19) was arrested here in 1915. Across the Clyde from Adelphi Street are, from left to right: the Boat House, Nelson's obelisk, the People's Palace and Templeton's (Doge's Palace) carpet factory. (PPC, Valentine B4241, reproduced from an image in the Anthony Duda Collection by kind permission of St Andrews University Library)

Glasgow. People's Palace.

The People's Palace, c. 1910, a Museum of Glasgow history, was one of several of the name in European cities, including London, as part of a movement to bring to 'ordinary' people the kind of 'culture' provided for the better off. Built in 1898, it houses a popular display of Glaswegiana with the Winter Gardens, said to be the shape of the hull of HMS *Victory* turned turtle, as a leafy place to rest weary feet, have a cup of tea and watch performances. (PPC, *Ingram Series*)

A demonstration in Glasgow Green on 4 September 1913, in support of Irish transport workers in their dispute about union recognition. Riots in Dublin had left two dead and over 500 injured, although the events there had had their comic side when Jim Larkin, the strike leader, out on bail, was smuggled into the Imperial Hotel wearing a false beard to give a speech from the balcony, while the Count and Countess of Markievicz distracted the attention of the police by driving past in their coach. No such goings on, which provoked further riots when Larkin was rearrested, took place in front of the 10,000 who gathered round Glasgow's Nelson's Monument. A larger protest meeting was held in Manchester on the same day. (PPC, Anthony Duda Collection)

The baker's van from John Dunn's Eastern Bakery at 274 Abercromby Street, on a winter's day around 1910, probably beside nearby Glasgow Green; all are clad for the cold, including the horse. (PPC, J. White, Oatlands)

Opposite: James Maxton MP, represented Bridgeton from 1922 till his death at the age of 61 in 1946. One of the last Independent Labour Party Members in the House, he was a much loved and respected figure, not merely in Glasgow. Almost uniquely for a back bencher, the Speaker asked Members to stand in silence when his death was announced and sincere tributes to his integrity and unfailing courtesy were paid from all sides. Churchill called him 'the greatest gentleman in the House of Commons'. Son of a teacher, he also taught until dismissed in 1915 for his political activities which had resulted in a year's imprisonment. Uncompromising in his politics, he was the most approachable of men and enjoyed life to the full, subsisting, it is said, on tea and cigarettes. While it is hard to point to any single lasting political achievement, his influence in crusading against hypocrisy, social inequality and unrelieved poverty kept these issues alive. He said: 'I am here to preach the gospel of discontent' - not, though, to preach violent discontent. He is shown on the golf course in about 1927 in the company of his son, 'wee Jimmy' and Campbell Stephen, MP for Camlachie. (Courtesy of John Maxton MP and the Glasgow City Archives)

The Glasgow Anarchists celebrate New Year, 1915, probably in their Buchanan Street meeting place - not that there was much to celebrate. A spin off from William Morris's Socialist League, they were active from 1903, promoting their opposition to organised government and organised labour. Best known, peaceful and persecuted, was Londoner Guy Aldred who settled here after the First World War. On setting up in the West End they called their place Bakunin House, after the Russian anarchist, Aldred's hero. Many of the men seen here would suffer as conscientious objectors when conscription came. Like Aldred, these anarchists did not slink around after dark, concealing bombs under their cloaks. (PPC, Stanley Hunter Collection)

The Olympia Theatre of Varieties at Bridgeton Cross, in the heart of John Maxton's constituency and venue for many of his meetings, was built in 1911. Here, seen when quite new, *Gorman's Juveniles* are top of the bill with *The Goodalls* in support. Seats cost from 2d to 10s. It became a cinema in 1924. Miller's Linoleum Stores on its right doesn't look much, but survived long after both wars.

Bridgeton Cross is a bit of the old East End which has kept some landmarks. The Bridgeton Umbrella remains as does the Olympia, no longer a theatre (*Sleeping Beauty* and the *Empire Girls* in 1912) or a cinema (*Elvis* in the 1960s) but a bingo hall. The van in the lower picture is Gilmour & Dean's - long established colour printers who had just moved away to Hamilton. The Tardis police box has gone now and the traffic can no longer circle the Umbrella. (PPCs, *Caledonia Series*, PN5215)

Bridgeton Cross, Glasgow   PN5215

The great Ingram Street fire of 17 August 1909. It started in a provision store at about midnight and quickly spread until the whole block from High Street to Shuttle Street and round to College Street was in ruins. No lives were lost and the fire was stopped from reaching the spirits stored in the cellars of Hugh Buchanan at the corner of Shuttle Street. Twenty firms were put out of business and the Albion Halls burnt down. Damage was said to be £250,000. (PPC, J. Bates, Baird Street)

The Royal Infirmary, built in 1904, replaced the more admired Adam building of 1791. It looks very clean, being brand new when the picture was taken across John Knox Street. It has since extended up Castle Street and round into Alexandra Parade. The railings on the left surround the statue of King William and a small boy is coming down the sloping path on a home made bogey with the initials SRCS on the side: St Rollox Co-operative Society.

Royal Infirmary residents (house officers) in 1914. Dr Thom, Medical Superintendent (with the spats) has Walter Elliot above him in the centre of the back row. After war service in the RAMC with the Royal Scots Greys and being awarded the MC and bar, Elliot entered Parliament at the 1918 election and remained there, with some short breaks, for the rest of his life, mainly for Kelvingrove. As a Conservative and Unionist MP he was successively Minister of Agriculture, Secretary of State for Scotland and Minister of Health until 1940. Churchill saw him as one of Chamberlain's men and he never held office again. He was installed as Rector of Glasgow University in February 1948, made a Companion of Honour in 1952 and died in January 1958. An honourable and well respected politician, he suffered a tragic loss when his first wife was killed on their honeymoon in a fall on the Cuillins; he remarried in 1934 and his widow later had a noted political career of her own in the Lords. Also set to make his mark in life not just as a physician, although he was a consultant at the Victoria Infirmary until 1930, is O.H. Mavor, better known as playwright James Bridie, on the extreme right in the front row. W.R. Snodgrass (fourth from left, middle row) and Matthew White (above Mavor) were consultants in Glasgow when fellow resident Elliot was Rector. (By kind permission of the University of Glasgow Archives)

The front door of Provand's Lordship, built in 1471, part of St Nicholas Hospital for the support of twelve aged men. Thought to have been the house of the Master, or Preceptor, it was the only part to survive. By the last century it had become an ale house and later housed other businesses, but has long been a museum open to the public. A medieval garden has recently been recreated behind the house.

Glasgow Cathedral, in an atmospheric picture, c. 1910, from the Necropolis. The oldest parts of the Cathedral are twelfth century. The graveyard on its sloping site has become a tourist attraction because of its varied and sometimes spectacular memorials and has made a good locale for ghostly or otherwise scary encounters on film. Sadly, many of the memorials are in need of attention. (PPC, Judges Ltd, 1893)

Two

Argyle Street

Most of Glasgow's civic and commercial centre lies between two long streets which eventually merge: Argyle and Sauchiehall. The latter may be better known outside the city but it was always Argyle Street, closer to the old heart of Glasgow, which exiled natives thought of when they were feeling sentimental. 'Argyle Streets' could be found in many odd parts of the old Empire, showing that Glaswegians had been there. About two miles in length from the Trongate to the Kelvin, Argyle Street begins to change after the Hielan'man's Umbrella, and later the tenements take over and a lone tree is seen in the distance. As the street cuts through Anderston it now gets lost for a while, but surfaces again near Finnieston. The village of Anderston, founded by James Anderson in 1725, was once noted for its Delftfield Pottery and Verreville Glassworks, heavy engineering, bakeries, whisky bonds and narrow streets of crowded tenements. It suffered some bombing during the Second World War and a major fire in a whisky bond later. Most of the rest of Anderston fell to the bulldozer shortly after. The Anderston Centre, a grand scheme comprising housing, shops and a bus terminal, which never lived up to its planners' hopes, has been renewed. At the far end Argyle Street opens up to take in the Art Galleries and the Kelvin Hall, beyond the scope of this work. Famed for shopping, the first part was once dominated by the Royal Polytechnic store and later Lewis's, whose building, attached to the great, glass St Enoch Centre, has survived. Saturday afternoon in Argyle Street has always been the place to see a cross section of Glasgow people. Apart from the looming presence of the Centre, the street here looks surprisingly unchanged from the 1950s if you ignore the pedestrianisation of one part and the fact that the old trams no longer make their way down the middle on their way from Auchenshuggle to Dalmuir West, and back.

Argyle Street from Trongate in the 1920s. Woolworth left here years ago and are now down by Jamaica Street. The tall office block past Miller Street now has Littlewood's store beyond it. The Argyle cinema, showing *If I Were Queen*, is just visible in the left foreground. Opened in 1910 in a converted roller skating rink, it finally shut in 1960. The shoppers are out in force and a horse drawn Glasgow & South Western Railway van is parked at the kerb. (PPC)

Argyle Street, viewed a little further west. John Anderson's Royal Polytechnic, the city's best known department store in its day, is on the left. It made way for Lewis's in the 1920s. In this pre 1914 view trams three-abreast occupy most of the carriageway and the pavements are packed - it must be Saturday afternoon. Above the 'Poly's' windows the name Adelphi Hotel is picked out in large letters. Later the Adelphi was at the Union Street corner. (PPC, E. & A. Schwerdtfeger, EO2326)

KENILWORTH HOTEL,
5 Queen Street, GLASGOW.
Telegrams: "Abundance." Glasgow.   A. CAMERON, Proprieto

The Kenilworth Hotel, *c.* 1910s, on the corner of Queen Street and Argyle Street, survived until the 1980s when it was replaced by a modern fast food joint (since departed) and office block, tastefully faced in red sandstone. It had been, before that, a good place to get an old fashioned high tea before a visit to the theatre or the pictures. (PPC)

Queen Street looking to George Square, *c.* 1924. The Hunter Barr building was restored a few years ago and is now known as Guildhall. Alex King is next to a steamship agent and A. Harris, tobacconists, who still have a shop in the city - in the 1930s they had twenty-one. On the other side Young & Sons, printers, display postcards, pens and other goods while next door Vogt & Sons offer help to those who need a pair of specs. A hairdresser further up the street is followed by a pharmacy with a pestle and mortar above the door. The street was once called Cow Loan. (PPC, Valentine, 91440)

Ingram Street faces Queen Street across from the Royal Exchange. A peaceful scene by George Washington Wilson before 1900, now all has changed, except for the Duke of Wellington on his steed. The Bank of Scotland's 1960s building is now on the left corner and the fine block on the right was replaced after war damage. (PPC, J.R. Russell, Edinburgh)

The Iron Duke has looked across Queen Street since 1844, with the columns of the Exchange behind him. Sturrock & Sons, Royal Exchange Square, well known hairdressers for long after that date and seen here in the 1920s, proudly tell that they serve 'the Queen and Royal Family.' Above them Wailes Dove promote 'Bitumastic', which 'Holds the World Record as an Anti-Corrosive'. Law, Dawson & Co., Ltd are at Nos128-130. (PPC)

Royal Exchange Square from Ingram Street, 1951. William Cunningham's 1778 mansion house had its portico and cupola added around 1830, after it became the Exchange - it is not clear whether the 'Royal' was ever authorised. After the war it housed Stirling's Library and became the Gallery of Modern Art when the square was pedestrianised in 1996. (PPC, Valentine B4222, reproduced from an image in my own collection by kind permission of St Andrews University Library)

The Square, c. 1910s, which was saved last century when plans to join Gordon Street to Ingram Street were so strenuously fought. The Gay Gordons restaurant was below the clock in days gone by. Beyond can be seen the William Porteous bookshop, here until 1996. On the bills beside the archway *John Bull* is advertised. William Porteous never owned this shop but was its first manager in 1853. He went off to Australia with the takings a few years later but the owners kept the name. (PPC, Judges Ltd, 6097)

Argyle Street at St Enoch Square, *c.* 1930, looking east. In the left foreground is Fraser's, the first of the House of Fraser stores, which in time included Harrods. Beyond Fraser's 'Manfield's Boots' are being sold from the Dutch style building, rebuilt by Kate Cranston in 1897 as one of her famous tea rooms and sold in 1918.

Looking west from the same point; projecting signs include that of the St Enoch Picture Theatre. Montague Burton, the 'Tailor of Taste', has a small presence beside Manfield's; later they would build in Art Deco style on the Buchanan Street corner. The 1879 Stewart and McDonald store, now Fraser's, is prominent. It is the 1920s and horse transport still reigns for local haulage. A schoolboy nonchalantly jay walks and a black man, probably from a ship in port, is having a stroll. The chauffeur stands and waits by the open car.

Argyle Street in 1960, looking east, and the trams will soon be gone. It's as busy as ever and Lewis's great store will be packed. C & V dealt in furs, which it was then every woman's ambition to possess. A van from Ware's of Hamilton is seen in front of a tram; their Silver Link vehicles were a familiar sight in that town. The St Enoch cinema closed in 1935 but its squat twin towers (centre) remain to this day, attached to the new shopping centre. (PPC, Valentine D5684, reproduced from an image in my own collection by kind permission of St Andrews University Library)

It was Exhibition year in 1938. Lewis's Concert, Sketch and Cabaret Party added to the celebrations. The big stores were well staffed and out of hours activities helped morale and loyalty. In Exhibition year this group would be in demand for concerts. (PPC, *National Series*)

ARGYLE STREET FROM ST. ENOCHS CORNER, GLASGOW.

The Buchanan Street and St Enoch Square crossing, *c.* 1914. Robert Scott, silversmith and 'Pearl & Diamond Merchant' is at the Buchanan Street corner; along Argyle Street is a sign for Rowan & Co. At the other corner, St Enoch House, is R.W. Forsyth, 'Hatters & Hosiers', best remembered for the Renfield Street store. Along from Forsyth's is Robert Stewart, silversmith, whose last shop on the site of the old Empire Theatre, in Sauchiehall Street, closed only a few years ago. (PPC, EAS E02334)

ST. ENOCH SQUARE. GLASGOW.

St Enoch Square, *c.* 1908, dates from the 1770s. The church went in 1925 and the site is a bus stance; earlier it was a car park. The Subway station is now a travel centre. Twenty years ago the quaint little building was raised a few feet when the system was brought up to date and the 80 year old carriages replaced. The Subway, opened in 1896, was cable operated; it was taken over by the Corporation in 1922, electrified in the '30s and renamed Underground on the principle that a name good enough for London was good enough for Glasgow. (PPC, *Record Series*)

The Square as a car park in 1948. The century old St Enoch Station and Hotel were cleared away in the 1970s to make way for a Ministry of Defence project which kept shrinking in size and eventually found a home further west along Argyle Street. The front of the St Enoch shopping centre now fills the space. (PPC, Valentine B624, reproduced from an image in my own collection by kind permission of St Andrews University Library)

St Enoch station was the Glasgow & South Western Railway (LMS after 1923) terminus. Trains via Dumfries connected with the Midland Railway at Carlisle to journey on via the Settle line to St Pancras, a service which lasted till the 1960s. A listed building, the delay in doing away with it after closure in 1966 gave it a further lease of life as a car park. The great arch is seen in its last days with the big clock still there at the far end. The fashions and cars date the picture to the early '70s.

Argyle Street in the 1920s. Brightly painted these days, the Hielan'man's Umbrella carries the tracks to Central station. The Argyle Hotel has since been rebuilt three times to be the Adelphi, Boots the Chemists and, now, Dillon's bookshop. On the left, the famous Queen Anne Restaurant was wiped out in 1951 in the fire which took away Arnott Simpson's store at the Jamaica Street corner. Mackay's Sparkling Kola is 'Patronised by Royalty'. On the far corner of Union Street an unhappy baby looks down - 'Give is Nestles' (sic) the sign reads.

Argyle Street where Union Street and Jamaica Street meet, in Edwardian days, and the trams and pavements are thronged. At Sherry's Shaving Parlour it costs 2d a go; you can have a haircut for 4d and then have the finishing touch from 'the most up-to-date hygienic hair brushing machine in the city'. Boots polished as well. (PPC, EAS 0185)

Union Street was the main tram route south from the centre. Glaswegians of all ages who wanted to survive had to learn to be quick on their feet when crossing here, and a fine example is the lady who has just dodged behind the motor bike and is making sure the Renfrew tram, No.571, won't get her. Behind her a young man stands to attention between the rails, hoping to get across safely once the Kirklee car has moved away, while in front of it another man can be seen jumping onto a moving Riddrie car, No.256. On a sunny day the open balcony trams gave you a grandstand view of life in the city streets. This is a fine morning, but seemingly windy as the girl on the right is having to hold her hat on - or has she just got a headache? Behind her, the cart horse is having a bite to eat. All life is here. Today, the junction is still busy with cars, buses and trucks, but not nearly so exciting.

Argyle Street in the 1930s, when the Adelphi Hotel was on the Union Street corner. Boots the Chemists are on the ground floor, 'Open Day & Night' as it says over the entrance. The tram is about to turn left into Jamaica Street on its way to Paisley West, part of the long route from Airdrie to Ferguslie Mills, an hour and three quarters ride for tuppence ha'penny. (PPC, *Herald Series*)

Argyle Street from Jamaica Street, 1963, and already a glimpse of a half-forgotten past. The new Boots' building and its big clock with the St Andrew's cross motif, was replaced a few years ago by something more traditional with a touch of Mackintosh. 'Boots' Corner', as it was long known, was a favourite rendezvous. This view was taken in the short interval between the end of the trams and the start of one way traffic. (PPC, *National Series*)

BROOMIELAW CORNER, JAMAICA STREET, GLASGOW.

Jamaica Street, from Argyle Street to Glasgow Bridge, c. 1910s, was a busy shopping street with stores such as Paisley's and the Colosseum, now both gone, and Gardiner's cast iron building at Midland Street. The Grand Central cinema higher up the street was latterly a favourite with the dirty raincoats. The Clyde Street corner, where James Brown sold chairs, piano stools and cabinets made in Dalmarnock, became the site of the Royal Stuart Hotel in the '60s but this too fell on hard times and now houses Strathclyde University students. (PPC, EAS EO2332)

ARGYLE ST LOOKING EAST FROM FINNIESTON CROSS GLASGOW.

Finnieston Cross, a mile farther west, c. 1920. The tenements have largely survived. Claremont Street is on the left and at St Vincent Street was the Anderston United Free Church. Finnieston Street itself, just off the picture on the right, is now a place of functional commercial buildings only, crossed by the Clydeside Expressway. It led to the Dublin steamers at one time and until the 1920s had a one man shuttle tram service. It also led to the old tunnel and Queen's Dock, where the Exhibition and Conference Centre now stands. (PPC, *Caledonia Series*)

Anderston House, at 470 Argyle Street, by Anderston Cross. A hotel which started life as the city's first Holiday Inn replaced it and then Argyle Street, as was, gets lost for a while under the approach to the Kingston Bridge. The stylish, red sandstone Edwardian building has King Neptune with his trident at the corner and other carvings on a watery theme along the front; an inscribed plaque in Pitt Street reads 'Neptune Buildings'. The Glasgow & Govan Bootmaking & Repairing Company shop has boots and shoes for 7s 11d and 10s 6d this sunny afternoon around 1909. The main part of Anderston House, however, was the Pitt Street Common Lodging House. At the street corner a barefoot boy is seen, a common sight in Glasgow until the 1920s. (PPC, W. Ross, 8 Matheson Road, Glasgow)

Three

Buchanan Street
and George Square

Buchanan Street has always been 'the' street for those shoppers whose hunger for quality is matched by the availability of funds. The opening of the elegant Princes Square mall a few years ago has seen to it that standards have not slipped. It was the one busy street never to have had the trams. Plans to bring them across the Clyde from South Portland Street in horse car days were fought off and the track on the other side of the river lay almost unused for over fifty years. Buchanan Street is free of all traffic now. George Square, laid out around the 1780s, became the main place for the city's hotels after Queen Street station opened in 1842 and still here, renamed, is the old North British Railway Hotel. The Square became the civic heart of Glasgow later after the GPO and then the new Municipal Buildings were put up, with the Merchants' House Building on the opposite side helping to give the city a most worthy and dignified centre. Sir Walter Scott, on his column, and other worthies less elevated, have since been a constant source of argument between the pros and the antis, to be left in peace, or to be banished. David Livingstone was sent off when an information bureau needed his space in the early 1960s and is now found near the Cathedral. Not even the Cenotaph is safe from those who want to move everything around.

The whole length of Buchanan Street viewed from St Enoch's Square in 1948. The stylish 1938 Information Bureau, left, was later replaced by a wooden hut in George Square. The Clydesdale Bank is just as handsome again after a recent cleaning; beyond is the 1930s Montague Burton store. There is a good view of the Macdonald Argyle Street frontage with H. Samuel, the jeweller, at the corner, where it was to stay for many more years. (PPC, Valentine B634, reproduced from an image in my own collection by kind permission of St Andrews University Library)

The lower end of Buchanan Street in the 1930s when hemlines were low. Across from Fraser's are the Macdonald and Wylie & Lochhead stores - now Fraser's! Wylie Hill, beyond Jaeger, was a famous place for stationery, toys, china and other desirable objects. Like many local firms, it died in the '60s. Stuart Cranston's tea room, there till the '50s, is at the Argyle Arcade. A magnificent Daimler waits at the kerb. (PPC, *National Series*)

Argyle Arcade in 1906, an L-shape from Buchanan Street to Argyle Street, not much changed since 1827. Brighter now though, its thirty or so jewellers make it sparkle. Many of the once-young will recall the Clyde Model Dockyard at the corner, where they bought additions for their model railways or fleets of boats or just gazed longingly at the displays. Mrs Diack's shop helped dress several generations of the very young in the best that money could buy. One ancient business that does remain is Sloan's Restaurant. The front of the building, reached through Morrison Court in Argyle Street, looked much the same when it opened in 1797. On Wednesdays, the day the farmers came to town, boiled sheep's head was the favoured dish. (PPC, Valentine 52825)

Number 91 Buchanan Street was the Victoria League Overseas Club in the 1920s, but from 1897 until 1918 was Kate Cranston's Tea and Luncheon Rooms. The architect was Edinburgh's George Washington Browne but Mackintosh designed the interior, with some of the fittings by George Walton, another celebrated local designer who soon after moved his business south. By the 1930s it was the home of the Clydesdale Bank and now houses the Bradford & Bingley Building Society. (PPC)

Buchanan Street is busy enough here in a late 1930s afternoon. A coal lorry is parked behind the van on the right outside Rowan's, outfitters at the upper end of the market, with a big trade in school uniforms. They closed long ago, but the building has since been renamed Rowan House. Across from the coal, Dunn's lemonade is being delivered - a brand you can still buy. 'Swan Vestas, The Smoker's Match' is seen advertised higher up the street, past the Parliamentary Road opening where the Royal Concert Hall now stands. (PPC, Ralston G9)

Buchanan Street, 1957. The *Glasgow Herald's* high arched entrance was covered up when the paper moved to Albion Street and has only recently come to light again. Simpson Hunter, the shop to the left of the *Herald* office was a Fraser-owned dress shop, rather select. Some well known names are seen on the right. In the distance, at Sauchiehall Street, is the square block which was built after the war as a NAAFI club and later became a casino. (PPC, Valentine, D2138, reproduced from an image in my own collection by kind permission of St Andrews University Library)

It is 1937. Walk-Over Shoes, left, may have walked off since and Thomas Cook changed hands, but Lizar's, opticians, has survived over 150 years. The Cook building was replaced around 1970 by an airways office clad in copper. The large domed building at the far corner of Gordon Street, built in 1887 for the Commercial Bank of Scotland, now houses the popular TGI Friday eating house. The spire beyond belongs to St George's Tron church (1807) in what is now Nelson Mandela Place. (PPC, Valentine, A5787, reproduced from an image in my own collection by kind permission of St Andrews University Library)

Edwardian Buchanan Street, with W. & W. Logan, the jeweller, behind the Kodak shop sign. Kodak had their own shops in the major towns and the design of the interiors was another contract for George Walton. Henry Burton, as now at the Gordon Street corner, has Manson the chocolatier next door but one. (PPC, *Reliable Series*, Photograph by Judges Ltd, No.1901)

St Vincent Place, mid 1920s. The extra width seems to give just the right touch of dignity to this part of the city centre, but it is like this simply because cabbies had a long standing right to a stance. Ladies and Gentlemen are catered for underground here, the Ladies now guarded by the black cast iron surround brought from the old Glasgow Cross Low Level station, hence the initials 'CR' that it bears. The massive block behind it, built in 1870 for the Clydesdale Bank, is followed by the *Evening Citizen* (1887) the Anchor Line (1907) and the Bank of Scotland (1869). (PPC, *Caledonia Series*)

The *Evening Citizen* was one of the city's three evening papers and was latterly owned by Beaverbrook. It ceased in 1974. T.L. Watson was the architect of the red sandstone building 'based on the best French and Flemish tradition'. (PPC, 'printed at the *Citizen* Press, Glasgow')

St Vincent Place about 1930, looking west. The bus is coming down Buchanan Street and those in the picture are passing the Clydesdale Bank building, still there today but without the decorative lamps on their columns, as seen in the photograph on the opposite page.

St George's Tron in Nelson Mandela Place, built in 1807 and seen here in about 1903, is a city church still open. From 1955 until his early death in 1964 at the age of 45, the Revd Tom Allan was the minister. Founder of the Tell Glasgow movement and closely associated with evangelist Billy Graham, he received the St Mungo Medal and Prize in 1964, as the citizen who had 'done most in the previous three years to make the city more beautiful, healthy and honoured'. (PPC, Valentine)

Jackson's Dog House, 89-91 Dundas Street, was swept away a few years ago. There had been a tavern at this corner since 1846 when James Anderson named his place Koh-i-Noor after the big diamond in the news at the time, a name kept till 1908. It became Jackson's Dog House later and was owned then by Scottish & Newcastle Brewers. Alexander & Sons are round the corner.

Buchanan Street station, closed in 1966, was never very grand but busy enough for trains to the north. An Oban express is setting off in May 1936. Changing trains from Central or St Enoch could mean a breathless sprint up the hill. Before reaching it you passed the bus stations in Killermont Street and Dundas Street, where Walter Alexander's or Lawson's double deckers stood ready to carry you to parts which the trams could not reach, like Kirkintilloch or Alloa or their Bluebird and Lawson's Land Cruise coaches might transport you to even more exotic places.

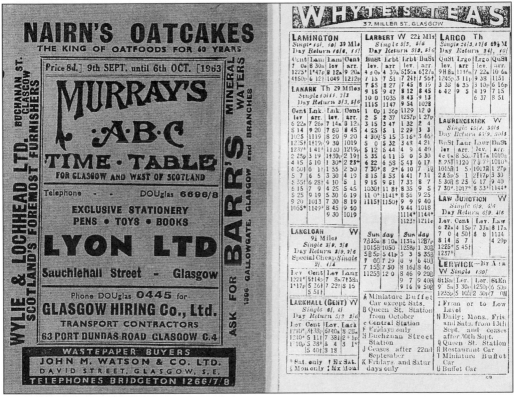

Murray's Railway Timetables, in their familiar violet cover, survived into the 1960s in the pockets of commuters and business travellers when you could get a train to a lot more places than now. Murray told you the train fares and also the mileage, as well as some bus, air and steamer details. At one time it was *Murray's Diary* with diary pages in the centre, but the tax people found out and wanted to charge Purchase Tax so it was changed.

21319. St. George's Square, Glasgow.

George Square, from the south east corner. Sir Walter Scott has gazed down on a few happenings from his column. None more notorious than on that sunny Friday 30 January 1919, when Willie Gallacher and Davie Kirkwood led a huge demonstration in support of a strike for a 40 hour week. It was peaceful until the People's Flag was raised, the *Internationale* was sung and unwise police baton charges started a riot. Over fifty people, including nineteen police ended up in hospital. Spellbound post office staff, watching from their roof top, looked down on charge and counter charge in what looked like a film set for an Eisentstein movie. The next day there were tanks and armed troops in the city, the strike ended and nothing like it has ever happened since. It is a part of the city's folklore.

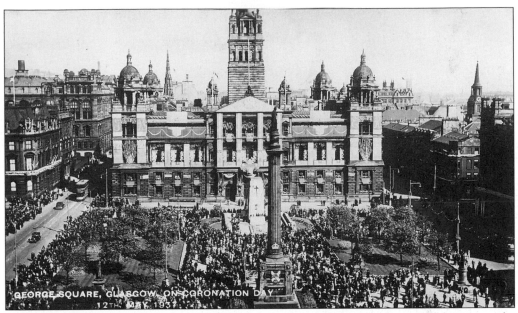

No riots on Coronation Day, 12 May 1937, just a great crowd to see the armed forces parade. Two thousand marched past Major General A.J. McCulloch, Commander of the 52nd (Lowland) Division, who took the salute. It was sunny, if not too warm. To the left is George Street, where a tram has just come out of the shadows after passing the Royal College of Science and Technology, now Strathclyde University. Cochrane Street is on the right and Hutcheson's Hospital spire (1802-5) is in Ingram Street. In the floodlit scene the royal monograms show up well, as does the city's coat of arms in the centre. In recent years it was Mr Happy on the front of the building, to the horror of traditionalists. (PPCs, *Herald Series*)

The Royal Hotel in George Square, at North Hanover Street, once had a fine reputation but closed long ago, to be replaced by a modern, out of scale, office block in the 1980s. This drawing is from an Edwardian advertising postcard by McCorquodale & Co. Ltd.

The Cenotaph was dedicated by Earl Haig in 1924. A Boy Scout and a Wolf Cub bracket a couple traditionally clad, he with the bunnet, she with the shawl. In 1994, Nelson Mandela danced here before the Municipal Buildings after accepting the Freedom of the City. St George's Place was renamed for him while he was in prison. More grandiose ideas for a memorial were mooted in 1919, such as a vast circular auditorium taking up most of the square, Glasgow's answer to the Albert Hall.

'The Tech' in 1914, as it was known by all before, and by some after it became the University of Strathclyde, has a long history. Named for Professor John Anderson and set up in 1796 as instructed in his will, the Andersonian Institute was a hit from the start. 'Jolly Jack Phosphorus', whose students enjoyed his practical demonstrations, was an odd character, often in trouble with his more orthodox colleagues. As the Royal Technical College it moved into the George Street building in 1905. The campus now takes up much of that street and Cathedral Street above it. (PPC, John Smith & Son, Glasgow 716)

G. Ferguson & Sons employed plenty of joiners to work on the new building for 'the Tech' in 1905. (PPC, J. Bates, 113 Montrose Street, Glasgow)

Rottenrow in 1908, an ancient street running from High Street to Montrose Street, means only one thing to Glaswegians: the Royal Maternity Hospital, where many were born and countless midwives and medics taught. The old building has been under sentence of death for years as one plan after another has come and gone. Three men wait expectantly by an entrance. (PPC, *Reliable Series* 4040/144)

Grafton Square in 1904, above John Street, between Stirling Road and Parliamentary Road, has long gone. It was a welcome open space in what became an overcrowded part of the town. Here now are colleges of further education surrounding a patch of urban desert. (PPC, *Grafton Series*, R.B. Johnston, 16 McAslin Street, Julia McLeod Collection)

Four

Renfield Street
and Blythswood Hill

Union Street and Renfield Street long formed the main north-south route through the city centre, leading straight down to Glasgow Bridge and onwards to the South Side. There was a good mix of shops, bars and eateries. In 1962 when the trams departed and the one way system put all its northbound traffic onto Hope Street, Renfield Street began to change in other ways. With four cinemas and a theatre (plus two more round the corner) the street had been a major entertainment centre but most of these places are no more. As elsewhere, the old local businesses nearly all closed and the booksellers' barrows were also banished - the Council thought they lowered the tone. West Nile and Hope Streets, on either side, were never main shopping streets. All around was the business centre, alive with bowler hats. All gone now are the little tobacconist-cum-barber shops with basement coffee rooms found nearby and gone too is the incomparable Lang's in West Nile Street where, in the bad old days, the businessman took his lunch and a drink standing up and only the bravest of women would dare to cross the threshold. Blythswood Hill is the steep slope rising from Argyle Street to Bath Street and that name is now to be seen on the new street name plaques in the grid laid out there around 1830. The gradients met when coming down, say, Wellington Street from Bath Street, never fail to amaze visitors. Such a drive by car is now actively discouraged. The original elegance of the town houses in the east-west streets can still be discerned in the offices, and many of the modern buildings fit well enough. Blythswood Square retains its dignity. Bothwell Street used to start very grandly and then petered out before joining St Vincent Street, but was further developed after 1945 in the style of any late twentieth century city, till it gets lost at the rear of the Hilton Hotel.

Union Street in the 1920s. Where 'Smith's Freebooter Cigarettes' are advertised is now one of four corner 'fast fooders'. Duncan's Hotel, originally a Temperance Hotel half way up, has been here since the mid 1880s. There too was J. & A. Ferguson's ('Nine Reigns') shop, a sad loss. A delightful aroma of coffee, cooked ham and fresh baking wafted down the street all day, drawing in custom to an Aladdin's cave of choice foods. The taller block beyond is part of the Central station. (PPC, Valentine 90401)

A 'white' tram, bound for the University terminus, passes Central station. The Ca'doro building on the other side of the street was at first a furniture warehouse, then a restaurant. Recently, after a fire, it was restored to its original plan, minus its criticised top storey.

UNION STREET, GLASGOW.

The top of Union Street in 1949. Gordon Street divides it from Renfield Street and R.W. Forsyth, the exclusive outfitter, is in the domed building; their Edinburgh shop was on Princes Street. Forsyth's closed in the 1980s after joining Tréron's in Sauchiehall Street - a venture which literally went up in flames. Next to it, Cranston's building takes its name from the Stuart Cranston Tea Room of 1897 and Cranston's De Luxe Cinema of 1916, recently restored as shops and offices. The tram shows the progress made in Corporation transport since the earlier views opposite. This was the last word in Glasgow trams - a Cunarder seen here when brand new. (PPCs, *National Series*)

GORDON ST. and CENTRAL STATION
GLASGOW

Gordon Street, looking across Union Street past the Central station canopy towards the Hope Street building which was meant to be an annexe to the Central Hotel but became offices and shops. The canopy on the right side is at the Grosvenor Restaurant, an opulent place whose famous marble staircase went during rebuilding as offices after the Second World War. The facade remains, the work of 'Greek' Thomson and his brother around 1862. (PPCs, *Record Series*; advertising)

MARBLE STAIRCASE. "THE GROSVENOR," GLASGOW.

Central station, built when the Caledonian Railway decided to cross the Clyde from Bridge Street in 1879 to compete on equal terms with the GSWR's St Enoch, was doubled in size in 1901 and is seen here in 1923. The Central Hotel was long the city's most fashionable but had lost that place even before it passed out of British Rail hands. The Corn Exchange bar, on the left, remains here; it used to be handy for breakfast when coming off the sleeper from the south. Tram track is seen in the street; this was lifted as early as the 1930s. (PPC, Valentine 90400)

Hope Street at Gordon Street, with Bothwell Street branching off on the left in 1904. Heaton, Taylor & Co. have their sign on the building facing us and the Norwich Union Chambers rise behind. All the buildings, or their facades, remain and apart from today's ceaseless traffic, it looks much the same now. (PPC, F. Bauermeister, Glasgow)

St Vincent Street, running all the way from George Square to Finnieston, from above Hope Street. The earlier photograph has the newly built 'hatrack' in the left foreground: 10 storeys, less than 30 feet wide. In the 1950s the basement housed a Craig's tea room, the last to be opened. Many of the other office blocks have long since been replaced. The later view gives a good idea of the massive style of the Bank of Scotland's chief Glasgow office, built in 1924 for the Union Bank. James Miller's building was based on the design of a bank on New York's Broadway. The Northern Assurance Company is housed in the tall block at West Nile Street. At the Hope Street corner, Claud Hamilton, a car dealer, advertises a fine range of names from the past on his windows: Arrol Johnston, Crossley and Morris. (PPCs, F. Baumeister, Glasgow; *Caledonia Series* Julia McLeod Collection)

The Bible Training Institute, better known as the YMCA building, was in Bothwell Street between West Campbell Street and Blythswood Street. A massive pile of Victoriana, it was built around 1878, with later additions, and was replaced by a modern office block in 1987.

Windsor Hotel, Glasgow   53776

The Windsor Hotel, on the corner of St Vincent Street and Douglas Street, was taken over during the First World War by the Ministry of Food. Rebuilt behind the facade, it was in the news a year or two ago when it was sold for over £10,000,000. Apart from losing its entrance canopy, it looks just as it did in 1906. It is now occupied by Direct Line. (PPC, Valentine 53776)

The St Vincent Street church (1859) is Alexander ('Greek') Thomson's best loved building. Externally it awaits restoration, but the Free Church of Scotland services continue in the notable interior. Pitt Street (blocked here) crosses Bothwell Street where for a long time the view was obscured by George & Jobling, who sold and looked after Ford cars. When they left a Habitat store took their place, the chance to show the south face of the church lost again; however, Habitat is about to move elsewhere.

Renfield Street, looking from Gordon Street in 1911. A brand new Argyll, with trade plate 'GD 1' leads the traffic. Drury Street and St Vincent Street open on the right beyond it. Parked by Forsyth's is a Delaunay-Belleville. The clock has 'CRANSTONS' in place of its numerals. With the horse drawn coach, complete with top hatted coachman, drawn up outside Galbraith's music shop, this view shows well the end of one era and the shape of things to come. (PPC, J. Crawford)

A busy Renfield Street in the early 1950s; in a full length view from high above Gordon Street it is busy with shoppers and trams. High up on the right side of the street can be seen the sign for the Odeon while beyond, were the Regent and Green's Playhouse cinemas.

A mid 1940s view of Renfield Street before the 'New Look' had taken over, crowded with shoppers on a sunny afternoon. The photograph was taken from much the same viewpoint as that on the opposite page, but thirty-five years later. (PPC, C. Richter, London, 84809)

RENFIELD STREET FROM WEST GEORGE STREET, GLASGOW.   A.8229.

Renfield Street in 1938, with the Odeon still the Paramount and the Regent beyond. Opened in 1934 and 1911 respectively, the Regent closed in 1982. The Odeon marches on, with lots and lots of screens. The Leyland bus passing the tram is No.301, built in 1930. West George Street was home to one of three Wendy's tea rooms from 1933. Though rather Anglo-twee, they were popular but like most others, melted away by the 1960s. No smoking allowed in Wendy's. None of the famed tea rooms of the past remain but a few new ones in the old style have since appeared, like the revived Willow Tea Rooms of Cranston and Mackintosh fame. (PPCs, Valentine A8229, reproduced from an image in my own collection by kind permission of St Andrews University Library; advertising)

RENFIELD STREET LOOKING SOUTH, GLASGOW   D 6475

A look down Renfield Street in 1963. The trams have gone but it is still two way. Some details here may induce nostalgia among the middle aged. The National Commercial Bank (extreme right) took over the Royal Bank of Scotland and adopted its name; Clydesdale (not the bank, but the electrical retailer) crashed in 1994, the Whitehall restaurant is a memory, as is Kirsop the hatter at the West George Street corner. Kirsop's - they sold other things too - had been redone inside in the '30s to look like an ocean liner with the floors called decks and in spite of changing hands several times since, some of the Art Deco look remains. Happily, the present owner is Cruise. The sign for Barr's Irn-Bru with the politically incorrect face of Ba-Bru could be seen all the way down from Cowcaddens, night and day, until he suddenly vanished when British Rail decided to increase his rent. Irn-Bru, though, is said still to be Scotland's second national drink; Tennent's lager, being unloaded at the Whitehall, may not be far behind. (PPC, Valentine D6475, reproduced from an image in my own collection by kind permission of St Andrews University Library)

RENFIELD STREET, FROM PAVILION, GLASGOW.

AN McCRAE, *THE GLASGOW STREET SINGER*

The Pavilion Theatre, *c.* 1912, near the top of the street, survives as the only unsubsidised one in the city, attracting an audience markedly different most nights from that in the other houses and having some great shows, with an emphasis on Glasgow wit and wisdom. St Stephen's church at the Sauchiehall Street corner was replaced by British Home Stores in the 1970s, to unite with the Blythswood church in Bath Street. To the left of the tram, a sign *The Impostor* tells us what was on at the Lyric Theatre.(PPC, EAS E02330)

Jean McCrae, Glasgow street singer. Outside the theatre there was always entertainment from buskers and street artistes, usually looked on with disapproval by the authorities. The street singer, with her tartan shawl, would start her career in the back courts, looking for pennies to be thrown down to her. One such, Mary of Argyll, working under that name in Newcastle, was 'discovered' and put on a music hall stage as a 'nightingale from the slums, singing to support her invalid brother' - a piece of pure invention by the promoter. After coming to Glasgow and marrying she became the mother of Jimmy Logan and singer Annie Ross, and the whole Logan family of entertainers.

Five

Sauchiehall Street (to Charing Cross)

Sauchiehall Street runs all the way to Kelvingrove, but mid way changes so much as to be something different altogether. Since the M8 cut across it the change is even more dramatic. The name of the street is said to come from the willows which once grew on the marshy 'haugh', so that those who say 'Sauchieha' would be correct, not careless. There was once a 'Saughyhall' shown on some eighteenth century maps on the south side of the yet unnamed road, and the evidence for 'Saughyhaugh' as the undeveloped land seems to be anecdotal, though equally apt. New building went on throughout the nineteenth century as part of the westward growth of the city, with commerce and business gradually replacing the mansions of the well off with this century's progress giving us the present rich mix of styles. People do still live here in the city centre though, with many more on Garnethill, no distance away up the continuing steep slope. Until the 1970s Sauchiehall Street had no rival as the prime shopping and entertainment street of the city, with theatres, cinemas, galleries and department stores a-plenty in or about it. Trams to almost everywhere ran its length. When they went away in the '60s that seemed an ideal time, first to make it one way, then to pedestrianise a chunk of it and plant some trees (not willows, though). But at the same time the big stores closed one by one, as did most of the cinemas, and Sauchiehall Street lost much of its magic.

Sauchiehall Street starts here. The view, from the dining room of Armstrong's Hotel, is westward; not so long ago a look east would have shown you Parliamentary Road but that has all but vanished. The Methodist church at West Nile Street, with its landmark tower, was a casualty of the 1960s. Between it and Renfield Street, the buildings, including the YMCA, were replaced by a square tower block, St Andrew House and its accompanying shops. (PPC, Edwardian advertising)

Looking east from Hope Street in 1933. In the distance Parliamentary Road goes off left at an angle at Buchanan Street. A.L. Scott had a chain of shoe shops. The Royal Hotel's entrance, left, is next to Annette's dress shop. Two trams and a bus are the only traffic; the bus, No.50, from AEC was Glasgow's only six wheeler. The YMCA by the bus advises, 'Don't Drift, Join the YMCA.'

'Looking east between Renfield Street and Hope Street in the summer of '57. Below the sign for 'Billiards' at No.98 are the Crown Salerooms of Morrison, McChlery, later taken over by Phillips'. Alexander Henderson, a well loved department store which made way for British Home Stores, is on the right. The No.23 tram is bound for Gairbraid Avenue in Maryhill. As can be seen, the smooth (and slippery when wet) granite setts remained in place in the city centre till the end of the tram era.

The Lyric Theatre in the mid 1920s was in the YMCA building and its closure, with that of the Glasgow Empire across the street, were both mourned in that decade of destruction, the 1960s. When trams ruled the streets this was the busiest junction of all, with its own unique screech from the four wheelers as they ground over the tight curves. One of R.S. McColl's sweet shops is at the Renfield Street corner; the chain was founded by the Rangers player of that name which survives under the present owners. (PPC, Judges Ltd, 11447)

Sauchiehall Street from Renfield Street, 1953. At Morrison's exclusive dress shop a motorist is examining the innards of his Morris Oxford. Fred Hill, jeweller, Crown Salerooms, L' Aperitif, Paige, Annette and Montague Burton take us to Hope Street, where the Royal Hotel then was. In the distance, past Dunn the Hatter, the Gaumont sign is seen. As the Picture House it opened in 1910 and as the Gaumont it closed in 1972, replaced by the Savoy Market, which took its name from the old Savoy Theatre (New Savoy cinema) in Hope Street. (PPC, Valentine B8433, reproduced from an image in my own collection by kind permission of St Andrews University Library)

The Wedgwood Room at the Picture House on a 1915 postcard. The sender, a visitor from Stourbridge in Worcestershire was not impressed with Glasgow: 'Rotten lot of shops here. Fairly big, but no size'. (Work that out if you can!) 'Streets are quite narrow and outskirts filthy. Rather disappointed with the second city in the kingdom'.

Top end of Hope Street, *c.* 1912. The Savoy Music Hall, left, (1911) was the New Savoy cinema by 1916 and in 1972, as the Majestic Ballroom, gave way for the Savoy indoor market, which lay empty for many years after being built. Campbell's Perth Dye Works had a national chain competing with the other Perth cleaners, Pullars, whose name is still seen. J.W. Smith was selling postcards - perhaps this one. A bill for the paper *John Bull* proclaims 'Grave Bank Scandal'. Horatio Bottomley MP, John Bull himself, was soon to face his own scandal. At Renfrew Street a blackened tenement building is where the new Royal Scottish Academy of Music and Drama now stands. At the top of the street the 1907 McConnell building, a red sandstone City Improvement Trust's tenement from 1907, escaped demolition plans in the 1970s. (PPC, Rotary Photographic Co. Ltd, 6372)

SAUCHIEHALL STREET. GLASGOW.

The south side of Sauchiehall Street from Hope Street in the early 1930s. Watt Bros., ladies' outfitters, left, not merely survived the retail revolution but still has plenty of helpful staff. Next door another Glasgow institution, James Craig's Rhul, did not last beyond the '50s. Craig's were all over Glasgow; the Rhul, and the Gordon were opened in the '30s, restaurants and function rooms on many floors busy to the end. The Rhul was noted for its Scottish paintings, sold off cheaply when it closed. Coplands' clock and the dome of Pettigrew and Stephens' store are in the distance; the latter's finial was seen again at ground level at the 1988 Garden Festival. The sandwich board man being passed by the Renault is advertising a sale of Railway Lost Property.

Bath Street was named not after the English city but for William Harley's 1804 public baths by the St Enoch Burn. A place of offices and churches, it became one way to complement Sauchiehall Street in the 1960s and has since borne the bulk of the westbound traffic. Much of the nineteenth century street remains, though not the 1887 YWCA between Renfield Street and Hope Street. It was replaced a few years ago and as Fisher House, No.80 houses red sandstone faced offices. (PPC, J. & R. Couper, Glasgow)

Bath Street's western end was well supplied with churches, three of which are seen here. The Baptist church on the left at Holland Street, still open, now boasts a restaurant, a creche and a guest house too. The tower at the Elmbank Street corner latterly carried a religious slogan in large neon letters but is now the site of an office block; the spire in the distance was at Newton Street. When first built, Bath Street ended at Elmbank Street and Bath Crescent met North Street lower down.

Sauchiehall Street in 1938 at Cambridge Street. Two well remembered shop names are Reid & Todd at 212, where many a handbag or suitcase was bought, and Muirheads, a Fraser store culled in the '60s. The No.5 tram is passing Marks & Spencer on its way to Clarkston. The Picture House was renamed the Gaumont in 1947. (PPC, Valentine A8827, reproduced from an image in my own collection by kind permission of St Andrews University Library)

The same view as above, thirty-three years later. The street has just lost its trams but Reid & Todd and Muirhead's are still here, as is Pettigrew's, with a new clock. In the distance can be seen the post-war NAAFI, which became a casino. It came down later and the Concert Hall and Buchanan Galleries shopping centre occupy that part of the town. (PPC, Valentine D6459, reproduced from an image in my own collection by kind permission of St Andrews University Library)

By 1965 the street is one way, with temporary signs overhead in the distance, directing traffic east and south. Glasgow's first big high rise office block, St Andrew House, gleaming new, is the most visible change. Grafton, a dress shop with many branches in the city, had the Victor Silvester Dance Studio entrance on this side of it. (PPC, Millar & Lang)

The department stores all had restaurants, sometimes more than one, and Pettigrews' Georgian had its grand piano in the corner like many others, a little light music being expected with the afternoon tea.

Sauchiehall Street, Glasgow.

La Scala, ('Only the Best Pictures Screened') in the 1920s. Until 1955 you could enjoy your high tea while watching the picture. The main feature here seems to be *The Merry Wives of Gotham*. It closed in 1984. The spinning wheel (right) denotes a John Smith & Co.'s wool shop. Beyond Wellington Street, Copland's and Pettigrew's lasted until the 1970s, replaced by the Sauchiehall Centre, not to everyone's taste, though the bleaker bits of concrete were clad a few years ago. Pettigrew's, like Copland's, a rambling, confusing place, had two parts (one built as the Fine Art Institute) with unmatched floor levels. Store loyalty was strong and regulars built up cosy relationships with the mainly middle aged staff. Both were near the top of the range - only Daly's next door sold more exclusive garments - but in the summer of 1963 a fire left a large part of Pettigrew's ruined and soon both stores had gone.

Sauchiehall Street, c. 1920. Charles Rennie Mackintosh designed the Kensington Restaurant as Kate Cranston's Willow Tea Rooms in 1903. In 1927 it closed and became part of Daly's dress shop. However, the original design survived well enough for restoration in recent years and tea and cakes can once again be taken on willow pattern crockery inside the shop of Henderson, jewellers.

The Rose Street and Blythswood Street crossing in the late 1930s. A 'yellow' tram on its way to Netherlee follows one for Langside. Until 1938 a tram's colour told you its route, a system which lingered on well into the '50s alongside route numbers. Shades were carefully chosen to allow the colour blind to distinguish them. The street sign Blythswood Street C2 on the right is a reminder that Glasgow, like London, had postal districts with letters and numbers until the post codes came. Unfortunately, some mail for C1 went via the Channel Islands. (PPC, Valentine A5913, reproduced from an image in my own collection by kind permission of St Andrews University Library)

Tréron et Cie (Les Magasins des Tuileries) a large, independent store, had no French connection at all. It still had its faithful clientele in 1986 when a great fire meant *la fin*. The news was not all bad, for the McLellan Galleries, behind, were protected by a dividing wall and survived almost intact. The facade stood and the whole place is as new again, with small shops and offices fronting a modern, restored art gallery. In scenes from 1924, the Rose Street end shows the westward view and the Dalhousie Street end looks the other way when the galleries were housing the World's Sunday School Convention Exhibition, and Treron was having its July sale. The tram, No.749, is a 'white' car going to the University. Most Glasgow trams reached a ripe old age but 749 was scrapped in 1939 when a mere 39 years old.

Sauchiehall Street, Glasgow

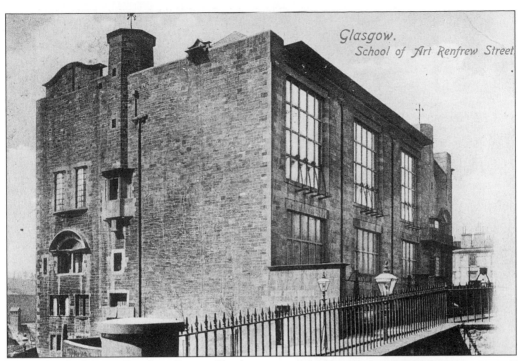

Glasgow.
School of Art Renfrew Street

The School of Art in Renfrew Street, Charles Rennie Mackintosh's masterpiece and Glasgow's most renowned piece of architecture, is seen in its uncompleted first stage in the earlier 1904 view above. The Dalhousie Street (eastern) aspect contrasts markedly with the later, Scott Street (western) one below of 1907. Building was started in 1897 but the front was completed only as far as the main entrance until funds were ready to finish the work in 1907-9. (PPCs, R. More, Hillhead; anon)

THE GLASGOW SCHOOL OF ART

SAUCHIEHALL STREET, LOOKING WEST, GLASGOW   B 640

From Douglas Street this 1948 view stretches to Charing Cross. Ross's Dairy had many branches. Art Deco influence is seen in Martins the cleaners and the Boys' Shop farther down the street. Today the schoolwear of 1947 seems as quaint as the name of the shop. The Regal, now ABC, where Ann Sheridan is to be seen, was later extended to take in the four shops on its right. The building dates from 1888 when the Great Scottish National Panorama opened. After the Regal is Alexander Thomson's Grecian building, then housing Blindell's, and a gap which was filled by the Dental Hospital in the 1960s. (PPC, Valentine B640, reproduced from an image in my own collction by kind permission of St Andrews University Library)

Sauchiehall Street from Elmbank Street, Glasgow.

The Elmbank Street corner had long housed Lyon, 'Society Stationers', still there in October 1968 when a runaway lorry careered down Garnet Street and smashed into the shop, killing one and injuring twenty-seven. Although Lyon's moved to St Vincent Street it did not long survive the disaster. There is now a block of flats here. The red sandstone building on the left remains intact; the gable end beyond is advertising Oxo above theatre posters telling of *Juno and the Paycock* at the Alhambra and *The Ghost Train* at the King's. (PPC, *Caledonia Series*)

The Beresford Hotel, Glasgow's most outrageous 1930s building, ready just a few weeks before Their Majesties arrived to open the Empire Exhibition in May 1938, caused a sensation with its bold Art Deco lines and its vivid red and yellow facade. Brainchild of cinema owner William Beresford Inglis, in time it ruined him. At first it housed Betty Beresford, a dress shop, and the Beresford Bar at street level, and the bar is back again. During the Second World War the Beresford was a favourite with visiting GIs and acquired a reputation all its own. In post-war days it was taken by ICI as offices and then became the Baird Hall of Strathclyde University. Alas, its bright colours have long been hidden. (PPC, *National Series*)

SAUCHIEHALL STREET AND BERESFORD

The King's cinema, 1938, opened in 1912 as the Vitagraph, ended as the Curzon Classic, showing 'adult' films. As the King's it did well enough into the '50s as a small, general house with a very good cafe above. On a fine summer evening it was a rare pleasure to sit out on the little balcony and survey the changing scene below as you sipped your coffee. Next door were T. & R. Annan & Sons, art dealers and photographers (now the Royal Highland Fusiliers Museum) with the Locarno Ballroom beyond. (PPC, Valentine A6696, reproduced from an image in my own collection by kind permission of St Andrews University Library)

Sauchiehall Street at Charing Cross. It is 1956 and the King's is now the New Cine. The main feature is *The Dawn of Venus* - we should never have seen anything half so exciting at the King's. The Locarno has *The Five Macs* and *Benny Daniels and his Orchestra* to dance to; no dancing here now for it is a casino. Penelope's shop front is in the unmistakable style of the time. The Grand Hotel stands in the afternoon sunlight. And the well dressed man or woman at the tram stop still wears a hat. (PPC, Valentine D2136, reproduced from an image in my own collection by kind permission of St Andrews University Library)

Six

Charing Cross
and the Park

Old street maps put Charing Cross where North Street faced Woodside Crescent, not at the Woodlands Road junction. Beyond North Street are the fine crescents and terraces which front the Park district, Glasgow's answer to Edinburgh's New Town, followed by streets of substantial tenements leading to Kelvingrove Park itself. The tone was set on the city side of Charing Cross by the Georgian Albany Place, but that, except for a hidden remnant, was removed in the 1890s to build Charing Cross Mansions. The great houses of the Park became offices long ago, but the need these days for modern high tech space may mean that more people could soon be living here once again. Perhaps there might even be fewer parked cars. Even before the advent of the motorway, Charing Cross was clearly where Sauchiehall Street's role as a shopping and entertainment mecca ended. South of Sauchiehall Street the tail of Blythswood Hill has its parallel streets running into Argyle Street but only Bath Street jumps the M8 to continue past the Mitchell Library as Berkeley Street, into a nondescript area of housing, ancient and modern. Woodlands Road runs along the other side of the Park district towards Glasgow's West End with a cosmopolitan mix of small shops.

The Grand Hotel, Charing Cross, 8 May 1888, and the are flags out for the Prince of Wales is on his way to open the International Exhibition at Kelvingrove. The people are out in force. Albany Place, on the right, would soon be gone. This was a row of ten identical town houses built by Philip Grierson, a jeweller (Nos1-5), Lachlan Lumsden, a lawyer (6-10), in 1825 and completed in 1839 by Robert Lindsay with a three storey tenement (11-13). Sauchiehall Street, a muddy lane, was widened in 1881 to give the elegant appearance seen here. Long hidden, the upper floors of Nos10-12 survive behind Charing Cross Mansions. In a recent photograph they are shown in use as offices, for a century invisible to passers by. (Above photograph courtesy of Messrs T. & R. Annan & Sons)

Charing Cross Mansions, left, *c.* 1905. The tree was the sole survivor of the widening. Several others were to be kept, but as the *Evening Citizen* of the time noted, 'it is to be hoped that sufficient wisdom exists on the part of those entrusted with the carrying out of this improvement to enable them to arrange the paving that the trees may receive the moisture without which they cannot exist'. The writer went on to suggest that this was unlikely to be done and that 'the consequences may be disastrous'. He was right; this last tree was gone by 1906. (PPC, Stengel & Co.)

The Grand Hotel on an Edwardian afternoon in 1905 - probably Sunday, as the shops are shut. Tram No.923, on its way to Battlefield, is the only traffic. The conductor is selling a ticket to a sailor. The shops include the Maypole Dairy ('Best Butter in the World'), their rivals Home & Colonial next door and Frazer & Green, chemists, all of which survived into the second half of the century. (PPC)

Charing Cross in the mid 1930s, viewed from the Grand Hotel. William Skinner's Tea Rooms, (right) as well loved as Cranston's or Craig's and of the same high standard, are at the corner of Newton Street. Skinner's was founded in 1835 and closed in 1961. Newton Street ended at Bath Street but the new Newton Street now goes all the way down to the Kingston Bridge. R.S. McColl's has a clock face carved above it, which became a clock again in the 1970s after many blank years. (PPC)

Charing Cross in the 1920s. Sir J.J. Burnet built Charing Cross Mansions in 1891, extending it as Albany Chambers later. Many of the city's public buildings were his and he is said to have been consulted in the redesign of the upper deck of Glasgow's older tramcars! A line of trams passing the Grand Hotel is followed by a bus owned by Currie & McGillivray of Lanarkshire. This was an earlier era of unregulated competition, with many and varied single deckers on the road.

St Georges Road in 1928, and Corporation bus No.54 is heading for St Vincent Street. Shops on the left include Royal Drooko which is closing due to 'Expiration of Lease'. 'Drooko', owned by an Airdrie man Joseph Wright (1849-1915), had an umbrella factory in Argyle Street and shops as far away as London. An oval sign (right) marks one of the salons of R. Stuart Bamber, 'Court Hairdresser', another well known local business which lasted into the 1950s. (PPC, Valentine, 204265, reproduced from an image in my own collection by kind permission of St Andrews University Library)

Forty years on since the view opposite. Not a lot has changed. The fountain remains, leaning to one side. It dates from 1902, a tribute to local MP Sir Charles Cameron. The post office moved across the street. The opening of North Street is seen on the right and the buildings this side of it remain right up against the end of Tay House, that remarkable office block built a few years ago on the mysterious bridge to nowhere. (PPC, Valentine D5682, reproduced from an image in my own collection by kind permission of St Andrews University Library)

Looking down St Georges Road from St George's Mansions at the start of Woodlands Road. Charing Cross Mansions is all that remains here now. Renfrew Street is between it and the 'S' curved front of the building in the foreground. The church seen through Newton Street was taken down a few years after the Second World War. (PPC, Taylor, *Woodlands Series* 12)

St George's Mansions in 1904, a grand, ornate apartment block in red sandstone, part of the City Improvement Trust's programme, dates from about 1900. Stuart & Stuart, the flagship furniture store at ground level, stayed until the '70s. Woodlands Road is on the left, St Georges Road on the right. James Craig's headquarters and bakery was in Woodlands Road, with a tea room, still open in the late '50s. The building, nicely cleaned, looks much the same today. (PPC, Valentine)

St Georges Road, near Woodlands Road. Cochrans' Furniture Warehouse, with '97' above, is where a cinema later had the Forth Bridge mounted overhead. A train was said to cross at times. The Q Club is there now, but no bridge. The other side of the road (below) now overlooks the M8. Next to newsagent Robert Adam, is William Teacher at No.144, then a greengrocer and W. Galloway, bootmaker. Ewing's China Warehouse is at Buccleuch Street. Young William Teacher, a Duntocher mill worker and ardent Reformist, planted the Reform flag on the roof in 1828 and was lucky to get off with a warning for what was a possible hanging offence. Later he opened his first 'dram shop' (never 'pubs') run on the strictest lines: 'No Treating, Smoking or Drunkeness Allowed'; a man before his time. This shop, one of the last, closed in 1960. Now part of Allied Domecq, Teacher's only connection with Glasgow is the city's name on the label. (PPCs, Valentine; Robert Adam, Gordon Carroll Collection)

Glasgow High School, 1905, said to have had twelfth century origins, was closed by the Council in 1976. The buildings (Glasgow Academy's until 1876) were soon put to use again as offices by Strathclyde Regional Council, itself axed in 1996. The new High School of Glasgow, run privately and incorporating a Bearsden prep school, Drewsteignton, is at Anniesland. The archway on the extreme right leads to the old Ear, Nose and Throat Hospital, last resting place of many a Glasgow tonsil and adenoid before it too was taken out in the 1980s. (PPC, R. More, Charing Cross)

The High School Council in 1906. Dr Hutchison has T.D. Miller and W.D. Glendinning on his right, with J.A. Stewart and A.S. McWhirter on his left. The front row, from left to right are: G.D. Henderson, J.A.D. Milne and G.A. Stewart.

India Street, from St Vincent Street to Elmbank Crescent, behind the King's Theatre, is now completely taken up with modern office blocks. Before these were built an elegant terrace made up the east side of the street, facing some typical Victorian tenements. More's Hotel, Nos16-20, had been there since 1912 and was the British Eagle check-in place in the days before you made your own way to the airport. The ex-Strathclyde Regional Council's headquarters was built on the site in the 1970s.

A view up Elderslie Street from Sauchiehall Street one evening before the turn of the century shows the entrance to the Park district. Not much has changed except that this stretch beyond Sauchiehall Street was called India Street then, confusing as the other India Street was just a few hundred yards away. The Park was developed in 1855-63 by Charles Wilson, after the University chose Gilmorehill as its new home instead of this site. The towers of Trinity College in Lynedoch Street and of the Park church in Lynedoch Place remain, although the church itself has been replaced by flats.

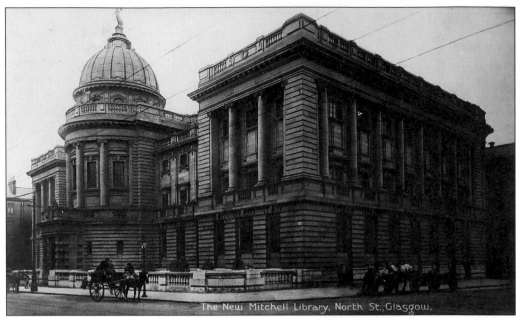

The New Mitchell Library, North St., Glasgow.

The Mitchell Library opened in 1911; the books, it is said, were brought from Miller Street by tram. The building was from a bequest by Stephen Mitchell, a tobacco merchant whose Prize Crop cigarettes were a 'hit'. After St Andrew's Hall burnt down in 1962 the library, which backed on to it, took over the whole site, keeping the facade and including a small theatre in the restoration. North Street, like St Georges Road, is now one sided, with a mass of high rise offices and hotels seen across the chasm. (PPCs, *National Series*; Philco, London, 4593/6)

St. Andrew's Hall, Glasgow.

Sauchiehall Street from the Grand Hotel, on a sunny afternoon early in the century. Newton Place stretches away on the right and Sandyford Place is seen in the distance on the left. The virtually empty scene gives a good idea of the splendour of this part of the street when first laid out (PPC, *Record Series*, Gordon Carroll Collection)

The Fitzroy Hotel, 1 Fitzroy Place, on the south side of Sauchiehall Street at Claremont Street, was one of many small private hotels in this part. After 1948 the building was taken by the (Royal) British Legion and as Haig House it is still their home.

The First Church of Christ Scientist, at 1 La Belle Place, was built as the Queen's Rooms in 1857: a concert hall for the newly developing district. It, and the stylish tenement block by the same architect, Charles Wilson, survive, as magnificent as ever. These days it is a Hindu temple.

Lynedoch Place from Park Quadrant, 1920s. The Scots Guards' Club was at No.12, Lynedoch Place. The Cameronians were also there, at No.4 and the Argyll & Sutherland Highlanders at No.9. (PPC, E.W. Taylor)

Kelvingrove Park, Glasgow.

This 1920s view across the West End Park, as Kelvingrove Park was long known, gives a good idea of the Victorian splendour of the Park district. Park Terrace on the right and Park Quadrant on the left, flank the wide entrance, by way of Park Gate, into Park Circus. Church and college towers stand out on the right and the spire of Woodlands church is seen to the left of Park Circus. The view also takes in Woodlands Road, on the left, with the houses of North Woodside beyond that and the factory chimneys of more northern districts seen through the haze. (PPC, *Caledonia Series*)

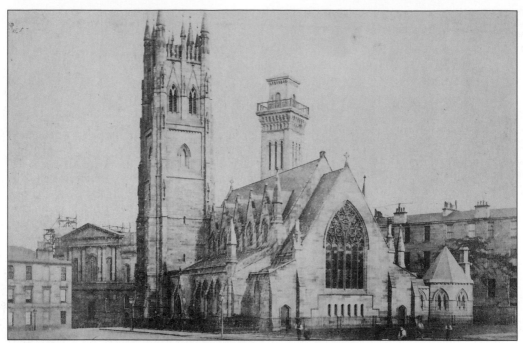

Park church, newly built, is seen here around 1860. It was taken down in 1969, but the tower, made into flats and painted white, remains as a landmark. The old Trinity Free Church College, here being completed with its two lesser towers under construction, remains intact, but has also been put to secular use. A few young cricketers play in the quiet street. (*Carte de visite*, H. Macfarlane, 107 Buchanan Street)

Woodlands Terrace, the site of the Glasgow Youth Hostel, with the Trinity College tower at the top of the street. (PPC, 351, reproduced by kind permission of the Scottish Youth Hostels Association)

Woodlands Road from Park Quadrant, Glasgow

Woodlands church, 1920s, for St Jude's congregation of the Free Presbyterian Church of Scotland, looking much as it does today, with Arlington Street opposite. A tram passes West End Park Street and a public house, now the Halt Bar and headquarters of the Lobey Dosser Appreciation Society. The statue of the feared Sheriff of Calton Creek on his two legged horse, *El Fidelo*, stands on the other side of the road. The pub was also a brief resting place for the Stone of Destiny in 1950. Unsafe houses at the other corner have been replaced by a brick building in matching style. Willowbank Street is on the left. All these streets lead towards West Princes Street, running from St Georges Road to Park Road. In the 1970s this South Woodside district was the site of determined community action which saved it from planned clearance and led to its restoration. Garnethill rises behind the spire. (PPC, *Herald Series*, E.W. Taylor)

Woodlands Road from The Guards' Club, Glasgow.

Woodlands Road from the Park in the 1920s. Above, the Domestic Science College is on the left, the side wall of Woodside School, since moved to Anderston, is in the centre with the roof of the Methodist church seen above the trees. The tall spire belongs to the Lansdowne church in Great Western Road. Below, the Burnbank Bowling Club is still here today. The tram is about to join Woodlands Road from Eldon Street, opposite Woodlands Drive. The spire of St Mary's Episcopal Cathedral in Great Western Road rises up behind, while beyond it can be seen factory chimneys and buildings, including Waddell's sausage factory in North Woodside Road. The Ruchill Hospital water tower is in the distance. (PPCs, *Herald Series*, E.W. Taylor)

The Bowling Green from Park Quadrant, Glasgow.

Seven

Woodside and Cowcaddens

From the start of Cowcaddens Street, by way of New City Road and Great Western Road, it was just about a mile to Kelvin Bridge, where you reached what was, until 1891, the Police Burgh of Hillhead. A little to the north of this route North Woodside Road and Dobbies Loan together stretched back in a shallow arc, now broken, to Parliamentary Road, through the heart of an area which took in some of Glasgow's poorest housing around Garscube Road. There has, traditionally, never been much space between the different income groups in what was, until modern times, a very compact and crowded city and in the streets and crescents off Great Western Road, roomy Victorian terraces and apartments were built for Glasgow's rising middle classes. There was enough industry and commerce here too, to support the numbers packed into the half-square mile bounded at its outer edge by the sinuous course of the Forth and Clyde Canal. The district was one of the first of the original twenty-nine areas chosen after 1945 for 'comprehensive redevelopment'. It was also, at one corner, on the route of the new M8 urban motorway which more or less took away New City Road and changed St George's Cross, a busy junction and lively shopping centre, into a virtual dead end. Of pre-war Cowcaddens there remain only the Normal School (now a business) and the newly opened Piping Centre in the nicely restored St Stephen's church. Many of the old tenements, though, did deserve to come down, and the destruction stopped before all was lost. Some prize winning new housing has replaced the slums. Industry, though, is no longer much in evidence.

Queens Crescent in South Woodside, between Woodlands Road and Great Western Road, with West Princes Street running throughout from St Georges Road to Park Road. The crescent was the first built here, in 1837, and streets of good quality tenements were added during the next forty years or so. It looks much as it was, if rather dilapidated. Drivers can no longer take short cuts through the district, making it a fairly peaceful area, but during the day it is one big car park. In this view from the 1910s, Melrose Street, off Great Western Road, is seen in the background on the right. (PPC, Robert Adam, Glasgow)

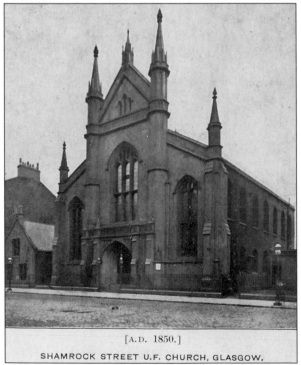

[A.D. 1850.]

SHAMROCK STREET U.F. CHURCH, GLASGOW.

Shamrock Street, parallel to West Graham Street, starts at New City Road and now goes nowhere. When this view was taken and until thirty years ago, it joined St Georges Road, where the United Free Church was built in 1850.

St George's Cross was one of the focal points of Glasgow. Coming from town you could choose: carry on up St Georges Road to the Round Toll and on to Possilpark, north west to Maryhill, or due west to the spacious suburbs of Hillhead, Kelvinside and beyond. Buildings here were of an impressive style and quality. The massive block fronted by four great columns (hidden here), housing Clarendon Halls, is now the only building of note. It was still busy in 1956, with trams clattering across the tracks in every direction and shops of all sorts with Fraser's, Wood & Selby and Duncan's and the St George's Co-operative Society's headquarters the biggest. The Empress Theatre, latterly Jimmy Logan's Metropole, up St Georges Road did not survive the ruination either. Massey's store had become one of the new self-service ones in the days when supermarkets were still only a cloud on the horizon - or a welcome gleam of sunshine? Now St Georges Road is the one through road between the stained concrete of the motorway slip roads. The M8 has a lot to answer for here.

The Grove Street Institute, near St George's Cross, *c.* 1904. Left is Balnain Street and the rear of the school in St Peters Street (Gardner Street then) from New City Road to North Woodside Road, for much of its life blocked by a builder's yard. Grove Street, wide and straight, ended in Garscube Road. The institute was an Evangelical Christian hall which had a big impact locally. Notices tell of the Annual Trip to the Holy Loch and of a chance to hear Revd R. Davies and the Welsh Revival Workers that night at 8 o'clock. (PPC, *St George's Series*, 114)

The Tabernacle, 56 Maryhill Road, opened 1894 and rebuilt 1907. It was inspired by Pastor David Jack Findlay, born in Glasgow in 1858 and, as his obituary says, 'born again in 1874, went home in June 1938'. Before the Tabernacle, his Mission was conducted in many places, including the Grove Street Institute. He was also active in the affairs of the Orphan Homes at Bridge of Weir, where he is buried. A special train was run to take mourners to the service there.

Butler's Furniture Galleries at 26-28 Maryhill Road, had not been long open when this picture was taken in 1957. Before that it was one of Glasgow's oldest cinemas, the Electric, known to all the locals as the 'Lecky' and one of the places where the legendary jam jar payment by young fans was a reality.

At Cromwell Street, Cuthbertson's in July 1957 was one of the earliest to go for a brasher style of shop front. 'Park Drive Cigarettes for Pleasure' and posters spread all over the place certainly brightened up the street. In the windows 'Biro Stylist' pens at 5s 9d each (28p) were not cheap by today's standards. Something called 'The Smallest Show on Earth' is in the far window. The Duke of Edinburgh tells 'the (exciting?) story of International Geophysical Year' on television - read all about it in the *Radio Times* - while Tommy Steele features in *Weekend*. *Motor Cycling* TT number is out and *Fling* offers an 'Exciting! Sparkling! Challenging!' read.

Lipton's shop in Garscube Road, 1931, with manager Arthur Parkinson and his staff. Special
offers on cereals (one whole penny given back) and 'Try our Famous Lemonade Powder'.
Hallowe'en Cakes, 1s and 1s 6d give a clue to the time of year. Peark's 'Holiday Christmas Club'
has the Ace of Clubs as a logo and the staff have it on their lapels. Lipton's, like Cooper's,
Galbraith's and Templeton's, later became part of Associated British Foods and the old names
have gone from the city's streets. Arthur Parkinson, born in 1908, is also seen opposite, fourth
from the right in the back row of the group of children pictured in Raeberry Street about ten
years earlier. He's the one at the back with the broad smile on his face and a 'piece and jam' in
his hand. (Julia McLeod Collection)

Wolf Cubs of the 25th (St Peter's) Pack, April 1950. They had been competing for the McNaught Trophy, a test of their Cubbish skills. Identified are Roy Chisholm, second from the left, Alex Dale, fourth, and Douglas Kirkwood, squatting.

The line of tenements is broken after Windsor Street and the gable end carries a fading advert for 'V.C. Pies - The PIEoneers - One Can't Leave Them Alone'. Eating V.C. Pies had nothing to do with valour; they were made by Vincent Coia of Queens Crescent at 91 Firhill Road. McDonald & Hughes show a nice lot of mirrors. Wee Murray beer is promoted by a boy who looks very like Wee McGreegor. Wm Murray started brewing in Kelso in 1880, but the Wee Murray came from Edinburgh and the company later became part of Charrington's.

Seamore Street, on the south side of Maryhill Road, in a view looking towards town in 1904. At that time this stretch was part of New City Road, which extended from Cowcaddens to Queen's Cross. The trams are doing good business and a third track is present as a loop for cars using this as a terminus.

Seamore Street on a Sunday morning in 1956 and the Salvation Army had an audience of about a dozen children, most of them round the fountain. A policeman strides past Gloria Gay's dress shop. Alex Munro had butchers shops all over the city. Past the the aquarium and pet shop is Dr A. Stanley Richards' surgery. The little 'lock up' surgery, open twice a day, was the norm before the advent of the health centre. The fountain, like much else, is but a distant memory.

The Seamore (an inspired name for a cinema?) was one of Maryhill Road's bigger houses, originally one of A.E. Pickard's. There were five cinemas altogether to choose from by the time you reached the Rio just inside Bearsden, and now there are none. This one closed in 1963 and was burnt down in 1968. Ann Sheridan is playing in *Come Next Spring*, with Sabu in *Jaguar* as the second feature. Waddell's sausage and pie van is coming across from Hopehill Road while the policeman holds up the cars waiting in North Woodside Road and a scooter scoots past behind him.

Ye Olde Tramcar Vaults at 246 Maryhill Road was famous for the model sticking out on its rails above the pavement. When the building was knocked down, the horse tram went missing for a while, but now it rests safely in the People's Palace Museum. The Lounge and Ladies Room were to the right, the family department to the left. Wm Barr was the licensee and Bass the drink.

The Blythswood cinema at Trossachs Street was one of the little local picture houses helping to make life tolerable for those living in crowded districts in pre-TV days. Apart from anything else, the back rows gave young couples privacy not found elsewhere, at a price within reach. Sometimes the film was good too. Doris Day and Phil Silvers were in *Lucky Me* in June 1959. Cocozza's Blythswood Cafe was across the road, handy for hot peas and vinegar or a MacCallum ice after the show.

Queen's Cross, where Garscube Road meets Maryhill Road, on a rather foggy February day. It is the mid 1950s but it might almost be twenty years earlier, except that the trolleybus has replaced the tram on Garscube Road. Since then both tram and trolleybus have long gone and so has the building at the gushet.

Maryhill Road above Queen's Cross, with Mackintosh's only church, St Cuthbert's (right). The Savings Bank of Glasgow, now Lloyds TSB, had a branch at Northpark Street in the building called Queen's Cross Terrace. The tenement remains here today though the bank and the No.105 trolleybus to Clarkston do not. Plans to run trolleybuses all the way to Milngavie were dropped when British Rail agreed to electrify their trains. A sunny Saturday morning in June 1959 has the shoppers out. A Hillman Husky passes on the left.

The 'furniture' shop at 650 Maryhill Road is a junk shop by 1959, with all sorts of bargains for sale from golf clubs at 2s 6d to chemical latrines at 50s. Studio couches, something no self-respecting household lacked in the '50s, are £4 10s and record players a massive £7 10s. The building has seen better days but the arcading and fancy iron work must have been impressive when it was part of a terrace.

The Forth and Clyde Canal, Firhill Basin. In its heyday a huge centre of industry was served by the canal, handling more tonnage than Glasgow's wharves. Law & McInnes and the Firhill Iron Works were still here in 1955. Millennium money will one day let us sail its length again, just as when *Fairy Queen*, *May Queen* or *Gipsy Queen* would take you on a cruise to Craigmarloch, past Kirkintilloch, for tea at the Dining Bungalow. Setting off from Firhill in 1905 is the *Fairy Queen II* which sailed from 1897 to 1912. By the 1930s only *Fairy Queen III*, built in 1923, was left which, with her three decks, looked as though she would not have been out of place on the Mississippi. In 1939 all this stopped, never to return, like many another simple pleasure, but some short trips are on, including those on a converted ferry boat renamed, of course, the *Ferry Queen*. (Below: PPC, Paterson's *Springbank Series*)

Round Toll and Garscube Road, Glasgow.

The Round Toll, Possil Road, going north under the canal to Possilpark. Another focal point has all but disappeared, with buildings swept away to leave a featureless wide open space. Edwardian days, but it looked just the same until the 1960s. Anderson Bros. promise 'Boots Repaired While You Wait' (it doesn't say how long) at less than 2s a pair. Garscube Road now is very much a place of warehouses between here and Maryhill Road. (PPC, *Record Series*, Julia McLeod Collection)

Oakbank (Western District) Hospital, built in 1904, just off Possil Road, fronting Baird's Brae. A trace horse waits to help haul a heavy load up to the canal. A poster for cruises is on the right; a board on the hospital gives opening times for the parish dispensary. Oakbank closed in 1971 but before that its spare beds came in useful when, in 1966, the Royal Hospital for Sick Children at Yorkhill was found to be an unsafe building and all had to be rapidly moved over to Oakbank.

Myrtle Street at the St Georges Road and North Woodside Road junction, c. 1918. Myrtle Street veers off left, to end in a cul-de-sac and Cedar Street branches off to join Garscube Road. This is a typical scene in poorer districts near the city centre. All was cleared after 1945 to be replaced by high rise flats. Smoke from thousands of domestic fires, factory chimneys and railway engines provided an atmosphere which gave the sun's ultra violet rays little chance and, with poor diet, rickets was rife in Glasgow before the Second World War. Wm Malcolm, family butcher, has some nice cuts of beef in his window on the corner of North Woodside Road and there are also two public houses to be seen: the St George's Bar on the right and another facing at the corner of Cedar Street. Allsopp's in bottle and Carlsberg lager to be got. There are two flats to let: a one room and kitchen and a two room and kitchen.

West Graham Street leaves Cambridge Street obliquely, and once met St Georges Road at the other end. Now it is joined by westbound motorway traffic. It runs along the back of Garnethill whose parallel streets contain much good housing of the style seen here, as well as some more modern. In 1909 Harvey's at the Cambridge Street corner has a notice in the window telling that it is moving in April to 353, New City Road, now part of Maryhill Road. Judging by the windows, they have already gone, but the cobbler next door is open. (PPC, Robert Adam, 146 St Georges Road)

Stow College, 1907, long a landmark in the Cowcaddens, an ancient street where the cows used to graze. The building was replaced in 1935 and the Free Church Normal School on the right, built in 1844, was taken down in 1973. David Stow was also responsible for the nearby Normal School. Oliver Cromwell came into Glasgow via Cowcaddens rather than the High Street, having been warned that an explosive reception had been planned along the latter. (PPC, J.S. Wilson, Cowcaddens Street)

Stow Street, Cowcaddens Cross (a grand title never used) was short with a good mix of shops, often busy with price-conscious shoppers from all over. On a wet day in 1958 a crowded tram passes by and a Ford Consul waits at the kerb with an HAC television van behind it. The Great Western Laundry van is in front of Crockett the ironmonger, an old established firm now in West Nile Street.

Wemyss Street had a zig zag course from Cambridge Street to Hope Street, passing the end of Stow Street on the way. By 1963 this old house was near the end of its useful life.

The Queen Arcade, Renfrew Street, in its last days, in 1960. It led to Stow Street. There was once a Wellington Arcade too, to Sauchiehall Street and when Woolworth's was built, the right of way was kept via the back entrance. The Renfrew Street entrance is supported here only by Cameron Bros. shop and the Camp Bar. The comically named tailor, West End Misfits, advertises between them. This section of the street is now the home of a hotel which started life as the Skean Dhu and, at the Hope Street corner, the new Royal Scottish Academy of Music and Drama. The interior view shows the arcade still busy to the end.

Eight

The River

The cliché 'Glasgow made the Clyde and the Clyde made Glasgow' is truer than most of such sayings but now that the city's role as a busy inland port is over and her shipyards, down to two in number, a chapter in Glasgow's history is closed. The river is no longer lined with slipways and cranes. The daily sailings to the Highlands and Islands, to Belfast and Dublin, the merchantmen and the liners coming and going, these slipped away almost unnoticed until all gone. Docks are filled in and the dredging of the upper reaches reduced. Only PS Waverley keeps up the tradition of a sail down the Clyde to Rothesay, Dunoon, and some of the few other piers still open. The puffers are an extinct species and the ferries went one by one when there were no longer thousands of shipyard workers to be carried. The vehicles were given the Whiteinch Tunnel and the Kingston Bridge. But a cleaner, though emptier Clyde can have new functions, an amenity to enhance the city's attractiveness, a site for riverside living and for leisure. Some of this dream is starting to come true. Medieval Glasgow was all on the north bank and the Old Bridge from the Briggate led to the village of Gorbals, or Brigend. The first bridge was built in 1345 by Bishop Rae and lasted, with repairs and widening, for 500 years. The Horse Ford, a little upstream, was another option at low water for long enough. The South Side, as it is always known, now stretches away for four or five miles in that direction. It would not be possible to do justice to that half of the city here.

The Albert Bridge (1870) from Saltmarket to the Gorbals, *c.* 1914. Of cast iron, it replaced one designed by Robert Stevenson in 1829, known as Hutcheson's Bridge, being sponsored by the patrons of Hutcheson's Hospital. Looking towards the city, Glasgow Green fronts the river with the old leather warehouse in Greendyke Street, and the mid-eighteenth century St Andrew's by the Green Episcopal and St Andrew's Parish Churches, seen beyond. (PPC, C.R. & Co. Ltd)

The Suspension Bridge (1851) for pedestrians, from the restored Georgian Carlton Place to Custom House Quay, on Clyde Street, *c.* 1946. Half-hidden behind it a small ship, the *Prase*, lies at the quayside. In 1983 the bridge became a feature of the Moscow scene in the television film *An Englishman Abroad*; the City Chambers became the British Embassy. (PPC, C. Richter, London)

An early 1930s aerial view. The Jamaica and George V Bridges flank the LMS lines into Central station. The original tracks of 1880 on the right have since gone. The bridge has no beauty and detracts from that of its neighbours. St Enoch Station is seen in the top right corner; the Adelphi Hotel is top left.

The clipper *Carrick* (RNVR Club) was moored by Jamaica Bridge from 1948 until moved here to Victoria Bridge. Built at Sunderland in 1864 as *City of Adelaide*, she took passengers and wool from Adelaide to London, once in a record time of sixty-five days. During the winter of 1977/78 very low water let her settle and her ancient hull was holed. Raised and righted with the help of plastic bags, she did it again and was towed to the Princes Dock canting basin, and a third trip to the bottom. She is now at Irvine, being restored at vast cost. The old building at the corner of Stockwell Street is here being demolished, ready for new flats, called Carrick House.

Glasgow (Jamaica) Bridge, by Telford. The foundation stone was laid on 3 September 1833 by the Lord Provost, the Hon James Ewing, before a crowd of 50,000. These three views show little change except in the traffic. It looks as congested in the 1900s as in modern times. In the early view above, the landing stage for the *Cluthas* (see page125) is in front of Paisley's store. Three trams are in line in 1937 - No.192, 'red' for Crookston, No.393, 'yellow' for Langside and No.1141 - on route 2C to Giffnock. This last was a prototype for the Coronation cars, built during 1937-1941 and generally agreed to be the last word in comfort in street transport anywhere. Their end came (except for four in museums) in 1962 and a No.48 Corporation bus to Nitshill is seen crossing the bridge shortly after, with a fine array of British-built cars. In 1937 the railway bridge to Central station was carrying a plea from the Co-op: 'Co-operators! Loyalty Pays - Develop Scotland- Ask For SCWS Productions at Your Own Co-op Stores'. Johnnie Walker and Lees' Macaroon Bars have taken over by 1963. (PPCs, Davidson Bros., London, 5019-6; *Herald Series*; Millar & Lang)

JAMAICA BRIDGE, GLASGOW.

A turn of the century view along the Broomielaw, so called since the 1400s and the starting point for countless voyages up to the 1950s. The old Renfrew Ferry lies by the south bank these days, converted into a performance venue in 1988; a bit further down the river is the *Tuxedo Princess*, a cruise ship which became a night club.

83   GEORGE THE FIFTH BRIDGE, GLASGOW.   J. M. & Co. Ltd
                  OPENED BY HIS MAJESTY THE KING, JULY 12TH, 1927.

The George V Bridge was added in 1927. Here it is brand new, in fact, not yet quite finished. The centre span is marked for shipping as the 'only passage'. (PPC, *Caledonia Series*)

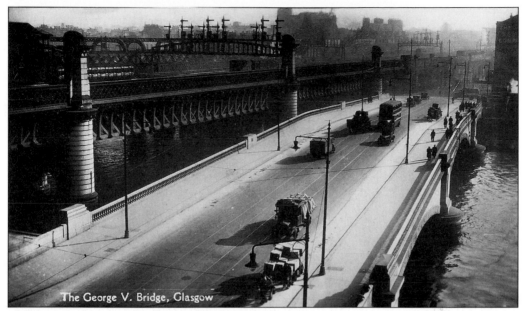

The same bridge in 1929, still quite new and not too busy on a fine evening. Looking south into Kingston, Commerce Street is directly ahead, crossed by Kingston Street at the end of the bridge. The dominance of the railway bridge is clearly seen. (PPC)

The evening rush hour in the late 1950s. The sheds on the Broomielaw are being cleared away in front of the Clyde Navigation Trust building and there is a poster for Red Hackle Whisky ('Scotland's Best') - a firm which ran Rolls Royce delivery vans. The 'campanile' behind that is a ventilation tower. The ends of platforms 11 and 12 of Central Station are visible on the right. (PPC, Valentine, D 2866, reproduced from an image in my own collection by kind permission of St Andrews University Library)

THE BROOMIELAW, GLASGOW. 537

Williamson's paddle steamer *Benmore*, built by T.B. Seath & Co. at Rutherglen in 1876, tied up by the Clyde Navigation Trust (now Clydeport plc) building. Her 200 foot long hull nearly failed to make it down river to the Broomielaw, being stranded on the weir for a while. Here, in about 1910, she is being used as a cargo boat and she was scrapped in 1920. The Edinburgh Roperie & Sailcloth Co. Ltd are behind. (PPC, *Ideal Series*, Davidson & Sons, Kilmarnock, 537)

THE BROOMIELAW FROM GEORGE V BRIDGE, GLASGOW B 7353

A packed *Duchess of Hamilton* is ready to sail from Bridge Wharf to the Clyde resorts, while at the Broomielaw is the Burns Laird Company's *Royal Ulsterman*, which, with SS *Royal Scotsman*, gave a nightly service to Belfast. (PPC, Valentine B7353, reproduced from an image in my own collection by kind permission of St Andrews University Library)

A CLYDE FERRY, GLASGOW.

Ferries, vehicle and passenger, were generally free. They disappeared gradually as custom declined with the opening of new fixed crossings. The Finnieston Ferry, when this view was taken, went from Finnieston Street to General Terminus Quay, but in the mid 1930s the slip on the north bank was moved to Elliot Street to fit in with plans for a high level bridge, which was never built there. (PPC, *Premier Series*, Lyon, Glasgow 2112)

Another old way to cross the river was through the Harbour Tunnel, opened in 1895 and there for foot passengers at least, until 1978. Vehicles used a hydraulic lift at either end. On closure, the tunnel was filled with sand. Handsome rotundas marked the entrances and the North Rotunda now houses a fine French restaurant. The photograph inside the dome dates from December 1977.

The paddler *Eagle III* leaving the Broomielaw in a daytime photograph turned into a fantasy postcard by an enterprising publisher to create a glamorous scene, a little removed from reality.

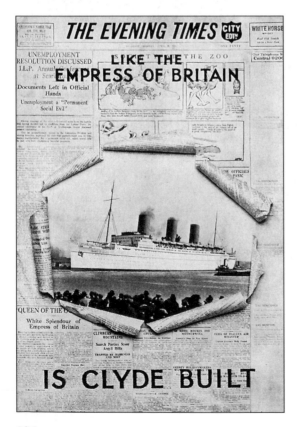

The *Evening Times*, Glasgow's one evening paper since the *News* and the *Citizen* folded. Easter Sunday, 5 April 1931, the country in financial crisis and No.534's hull rusting on the stocks, it was certainly a matter for celebration when the *Empress of Britain* sailed away from John Brown's yard 'to set out on the first lap of her Empire cruise'. First she was bound for Liverpool to have her bottom scraped. The pride of the CPR fleet, 42,500 tons, she was given a send off by around 750,000 Clydesiders lining the banks for 17 miles. She met her end in 1940, bombed and sunk off the coast of Ireland. The post-war *Empress* came from Fairfield's yard in 1955. (PPC, advertising, reproduced by kind permission of Caledonian Newspapers Limited)

The *Cluthas* (Clutha meaning Clyde) gave a water bus sevice on the river from 1884 to 1903, when competition from the new electric trams was too much for them. Many survived for years on other duties, some in distant waters. This postcard was published by J.W. Junr as a farewell tribute.

The Clyde River Patrol, 'G' Crew, 'L' Section, an arm of the RN Patrol Service, based in Lowestoft. Reservists and volunteer yachtsmen kept a look out for mines and unexploded bombs between Glasgow and the Tail of the Bank. The patrol was based at HMS *Spartiate*, the St Enoch Hotel, taken over by the Navy. The crew are sporting their new uniforms and silver RN Patrol Service cap badges, just issued in May 1940, and looking very spruce in their motor launch.

The newly built Kingston Bridge seen from the stern of the turbine steamer *Queen Mary* on a summer morning in 1981 (left) and a view up the Clyde from the bow at the end of the cruise (below). The end of an era too, for soon afterwards this fine ship went south to the Thames. She was built in 1933 and had *II* added to her name at Cunard White Star's request, in case anyone confused her with another ship of that name (John Brown's 534) about to go into service. She dropped the suffix when her namesake tied up at Palm Beach. From the bow the granaries in Partick are seen by a busy Meadowside Quay and Fairfield's cranes are on the starboard side.